The First Y

WILLIAM BUTLER YEATS was born in ████ ████, artist, and Susan Pollexfen. His famil ████████ Ireland. He spent his childhood in London, Dublin and Sligo. He trained as an artist, enrolling at the Metropolitan School of Art in Dublin in 1884. His lifelong interest in esoteric traditions found early expression in his membership of the Hermetic Order of the Golden Dawn from 1890. Yeats espoused the cause of Irish national liberation, and he was the most significant figure in the Irish literary and dramatic revival, being founder-president of the Irish National Dramatic Society (1902), which was the basis for the Abbey Theatre (1904). His early poetry followed Romantic and Victorian models, but in the early years of the twentieth century he developed a clearer and more direct style. His later poems are counted among the major achievements of modern poetry in English. After the establishment of the Irish Free State in 1922, he became a senator. He won the Nobel Prize for Literature in 1923. Yeats died in France in 1939.

EDWARD LARRISSY studied English at Oxford, where he read for a DPhil on the poetry of William Blake. He has taught at the universities of Warwick and Keele, and has been Professor of English Literature and Head of School at the University of Leeds, where he won funding for a major project on Leeds Poetry. As Professor of Poetry at Queen's University, Belfast, he plays an active role in the Seamus Heaney Centre for Poetry, to which he is affiliated. He has published widely on poetry, including on the work of Yeats, and writes poetry himself. He has given invited papers in, among other places, Oxford, Cambridge, London, Strasbourg, Kyoto, South Carolina, and at the Yeats International Summer School in Sligo.

Fyfield*Books* aim to make available some of the great classics of British and European literature in clear, affordable formats, and to restore often neglected writers to their place in literary tradition.

Fyfield*Books* take their name from the Fyfield elm in Matthew Arnold's 'Scholar Gypsy' and 'Thyrsis'. The tree stood not far from the village where the series was originally devised in 1971.

Roam on! The light we sought is shining still.
Dost thou ask proof? Our tree yet crowns the hill,
Our Scholar travels yet the loved hill-side

from 'Thyrsis'

The First Yeats

Poems by W.B. Yeats, 1889–1899

Unrevised texts, edited with an introduction by
EDWARD LARRISSY

Fyfield*Books*

CARCANET

Acknowledgements

I wish to acknowledge the great helpfulness of the staff of Special Collections in the Libraries of Trinity College, Dublin and Queen's University, Belfast. I am also grateful to colleagues and students at the Yeats International Summer School, Sligo, in 2007 and 2009, and to my students at Queen's.

First published in Great Britain in 2010 by
Carcanet Press Limited
Alliance House
Cross Street
Manchester M2 7AQ

A CIP catalogue record for this book is available from the British Library
ISBN 978 1 85754 995 9

The publisher acknowledges financial assistance from Arts Council England

Typeset by XL Publishing Services, Tiverton
Printed and bound in England by SRP Ltd, Exeter

Contents

Introduction

There is a widespread assumption that the Yeats of the nineteenth century – roughly the Yeats of the years between *The Wanderings of Oisin and Other Poems* (1889) and *The Wind Among the Reeds* (1899) – is markedly different from the Yeats who succeeds him. This early Yeats is late-Romantic in matter and manner, whereas middle and late Yeats are thought to be modernist, despite the continuation of certain Romantic themes and techniques. There is, in fact, much to be said for this oft-repeated account. Yeats was born in 1865, and thus his formative years as a poet necessarily passed in a context where the Romantics were living influences, still capable of suggesting new creative ideas. One, in particular, was still being discovered: namely, William Blake. Yeats himself, with his friend Edwin Ellis, brought out the first serious edition of Blake, the three-volume *Works of William Blake* (1893). His thought is clearly indebted to Blake's, perhaps most obviously in his deployment of the principle of contrary states, and in the related matter of exploiting esoteric symbolism for poetic purposes. But Shelley, with his yearning for 'Intellectual Beauty', and his rarefied blend of symbolism and mental association, was perhaps a more potent influence on Yeats's style. Alongside these figures, we must not forget the intervening years: Tennyson and the pre-Raphaelites (in particular William Morris) all leave their mark, in one way or another, on the early Yeats. So do a number of Irish poets who attempted to give new and living shape to the matter of Ireland through the medium of the English language, and in forms influenced by British Romanticism. Yeats himself, in his 'Apologia Addressed to Ireland in the Coming Days' (later to be renamed as 'To Ireland in the Coming Times'), identifies the Irish poets Thomas Davis (1814–45), James Clarence Mangan (1803–49) and Sir Samuel Ferguson (1810–86) as having particular significance for him. Then there is the question of French symbolism, which certainly must not be divorced from its origins in Romanticism. Baudelaire, for instance, thought of himself as a Romantic poet, though he is usually nowa-days classified as a symbolist poet. It was Yeats's friend Arthur Symons who was responsible for introducing Yeats to the work of the French symbolist poets, from 1893 or thereabouts, the year when Symons himself brought Verlaine to London. Verlaine's prescription, in 'Art poétique', for musical suggestiveness in poetry is probably an influence on the poems Yeats wrote from the mid-nineties onwards.

After 1900, and certainly from *In the Seven Woods* (1907), Yeats's style begins to change. The directness, as of a person addressing the reader, albeit with considerable artifice, has few precedents in the earlier verse. The tone and subject-matter also change. A neat way of gauging these developments is to compare and contrast 'Aedh Wishes for the Cloths of Heaven' (as it was entitled in the first edition of *The Wind Among the Reeds*) with 'A Coat', from *Responsibilities* (1914). In the former, the speaker spreads his 'embroidered' cloths of dreams under the mistress's feet. In the latter he speaks of how he made his song a coat 'Covered with embroi-deries / Out of old mythologies': it fares ill in the world's hands. In the last lines, the bitter contempt, born of disillusionment, is not uncharacteristic of middle and later Yeats: 'Song, let them take it, / For there's more enterprise / In walking naked.' The nakedness is that of an unadorned style and outlook, free of illusions.

There is only one problem with the account given so far, and it is perhaps not an insuperable one. It arises out of the contemporary realisation that 'Romanticism' is by no means the unified phenom-enon that word might seem to imply. If one only considers poetry, one should note that this word has to comprise the Romantic neoclassicism of Keats's 'Ode on a Grecian Urn', as well as the satir-ical point, sceptical humour and neoclassical style of Byron's *Don Juan*. If it can include these things, can it not include the later Yeats, as well as the earlier? In particular, can it not also include the Yeats who reflects, at the end of 'Among School Children', on the power of images in our lives, most of all those images where the life and the form are one: images such as those of the tree or the dancer? Are these not images in the Romantic tradition of 'organic form'? Frank Kermode, in his classic critical work *Romantic Image*, certainly thought so. But to let these considerations cause anxiety about terms is probably a waste of energy when the terms are so large and inexact in any case. For that matter, 'modernism' is as diverse as 'Romanticism'. Nevertheless, to realise that Yeats's 'Romanticism' does not disappear in 1899 is also to realise that there are likely to be important continuities, and that the early work is clearly essential for an understanding of the later.

Yet it would be doing the early work a grave disservice to reduce it to ancillary status in relation to the later. It is still possible to come across readers who deride the supposedly vague dreaminess of early Yeats as if this were a given of critical discourse. Presumably they have never analysed the techniques of a poem such as 'The Song of Wandering Aengus'. Here the speaker goes out to a hazel wood, a mysterious place full of trees which in Irish tradition were beneficently magical. He does so at twilight, and he is beside a stream. Symbolically he is close to both temporal and spatial boundaries, and these might operate like cracks in the fabric of the universe through which the supernatural might intervene. When he cuts and peels a hazel wand, to turn it into a fishing rod, that wand does indeed have magical associations, so that when the fish he catches turns into a 'glimmering girl' we should not be entirely surprised. In any case, she is one of the 'Sidhe' (the fairies), and a woman of the Sidhe might well be able to turn herself into a fish and back again. Appropriately enough, she is associated with the element of water, whose mutability might figure the feminine, and the speaker is associated with the masculine element of fire, which burns as the desire in his head. When she calls him by his name, this in itself is an act of magical power, for no one has revealed it to her. She turns the tables on his evocation of her, and now he must pursue her forever. When he finds her, they will, he thinks, 'pluck till time and times are done, / The silver apples of the moon, / The golden apples of the sun.' The elements of water and fire, which seemed so irreconcilable, are here transformed by the alchemy of love into silver and golden apples. The great lights of moon and sun represent the two major aspects of the world of time transfigured. This would be the consummation of a first meeting that occurred at a point where those aspects meet: at twilight. The poem embodies these ideas by the suggestive combination of images, and through a complex network of related sounds, and it enacts the desire of the speaker by means of an insistent, driving rhythm. To mention some of the ways in which images and sounds work together: for example, 'white moths' are out in the twilight of the morning, while almost next to them, you might think, 'moth-like stars are flickering out'. The combination intensifies the visual impression, and helps to convey more forcefully the important notion of uncertain apprehension. This 'flickering', so redolent of the 'Celtic Twilight', a time and a state for supernatural occurrences, is reinforced by the 'glimmering' that qualifies the girl, and the 'brightening' of the air. There is also a kind of auditory flickering: 'something rustled on the floor'. When the lovers are united in a land beyond time, the 'dappled' grass is a transmutation of the early flickering, intensified by its internal near rhyme with 'apples'.

Such is the supposed vagueness and dreaminess of Yeats's early poetic. There is more to say, of course, about his intellectual pre-occupations, of which this beautiful poem is in part the result. Of particular importance are Celticism, and magic. The woman of the Sidhe is a notable instance of Yeats's fascination with these denizens of Irish mythology and folklore. The poem memorably evokes the uncanniness of these beings, immortal creatures who live in a land beyond the western sea, Tír na nÓg ('The Land of the Young', i.e., of those who do not age). They may also live in hills, or at the bottom of lakes and rivers, as the 'glimmering girl' perhaps does. They may possess great beauty, and are not normally diminutive in size, despite the fact that they were often called in English 'the fairies'. Their beauty may entice mortals, and indeed they appear to wish to entrap, steal or kidnap human kind. Notoriously, this applies to children, as in Yeats's poem 'The Stolen Child'. But who can say whether or not they are really malevolent? Niam, in 'The Wanderings of Oisin', does not appear so. Yet the subtitle of the first version to appear in book form (which of course is what is reprinted here), is 'And How a Demon Trapped Him' – referring to how she enticed Oisin into the other world. And when we turn to *The Wind Among the Reeds* (1899), we note that Niamh (the same as Niam) is calling 'Away, come away'. In a piece of pre-Raphaelite eroticism, she evokes the heaving breasts, gleaming eyes and parted lips of herself and the other fairy women. Yet perversely, she goes on to assert that 'if any gaze on our rushing band, / We come between him and the deed of his hand, / We come between him and the hope of his heart.' Nor had all that many years passed between the publication of *Oisin* and the writing, in 1893, of this poem, so it is not easy to assert some change of attitude on Yeats's part. Here and in his subsequent work he involves the Sidhe in his meditation on a fundamental problem of human experience: our longings for beauty and truth lead us to wonder if these qualities possess such universality that they are eternal. Yet life is changeable and doomed to mortality. In his later years, Yeats turns also to neo-Platonic philosophy and to Romantic poems such as Keats's Odes for illumination of this predicament, but the Sidhe are never far from his mind.

But while they are the most captivating examples of the subject-matter of Irish romance, one must not forget the more general cultural-nationalist motivation which led Yeats to offer his powerful reinterpretations of Celtic mythology and tradition. Of course, he was a major figure in the Irish literary and dramatic revival. But this movement did not arise suddenly in the nineties, and Yeats always presents himself as continuing the work of previous Irish poets who had themselves attempted to reinvent Gaelic tradition in a contemporary English-language poetic idiom. For instance, in 'Apologia Addressed to Ireland in the Coming Days', he counts himself one 'With Davis, Mangan, Ferguson': i.e., with the poets Thomas Davis, James Clarence Mangan and Sir Samuel Ferguson. Yet there is more to it than that. Yeats's own poetic *début* is to be found in *The Wanderings of Oisin and Other Poems* (1899). The subject-matter of the title poem shows Yeats boldly handling the most celebrated Celtic material, namely the story of Oisin (or Ossian). It was James Macpherson (1736–96) who had first made the world aware of the name of this legendary ancient bard in prose 'translations' from Scottish Gaelic verses he claimed to have discovered. The first of a number of works of Ossian he published was *Fingal* (1761). Despite questions about the veracity of Macpherson's claims, and about his grasp of the traditions surrounding Ossian, his works enjoyed the most extraordinary popularity and influence down to the end of the nineteenth century. Coleridge and Whitman counted themselves as admirers, and the poems were translated into the major European languages.

It was Irish scholars and poets who tended to offer the most informed criticism of Macpherson's endeavours. Stories of Oisin were the common property of the Gaelic-speaking people of Ireland and Scotland. But wherever the tale was told, there was no doubt about the usual setting: Ireland. Ireland's attempt to wrest Ossian back from Scotland was most ambitiously embodied in the Ossianic Society of Dublin, founded in 1853, whose learned *Transactions* Yeats studied. In other words, Yeats learnt from a scholarly tradition instigated by Macpherson's celebrated work; and he also chose to base his first ambitious long poem on the matter which was most clearly related in the public mind to the essential qualities of the Celt.

These qualities had to do with the melancholy of lamenting a heroic age that had passed, and with a sense of noble but inevitable defeat. In his influential lectures, *On Celtic Literature* (well known to Yeats), Matthew Arnold had quoted (or slightly misquoted) a line from Macpherson's *Ossian*: 'They went forth to the battle but they always fell'. This sense that the Celts were destined to defeat by the modern world became something of a truism. It might be a badge of honour for those like Yeats who felt that the 'Grey Truth' of the modern world – its scientific rationalism and submission to the fatal disciplines of industry – had turned its back on the most profound truths about human imagination. Yeats gave as a title to one of his poems the same misquotation from Macpherson, and so it appears in this edition, though he later changed it to 'The Rose of Battle'. His interest in Macpherson did not survive into the twentieth century; but it has been too little considered that his oft-expressed regret for the passing of an older heroic order may owe some of its origins to the continued influence of Macpherson's Ossian into the late nineteenth century.

What the Celts actually believed, or may have believed, was also a matter of interest to Yeats, and the answer was thought to be well enough known. We need turn no further than to the final lines of his own 'Fergus and the Druid':

> I have been many things –
> A green drop in the surge, a gleam of light
> Upon a sword, a fir-tree on a hill,
> An old slave grinding at a heavy quern,
> A king sitting upon a chair of gold […]

Such ideas about transmigration of souls – and indeed about a priesthood who taught them – supported the long-held notion that the

Celts (including the Irish) were of oriental origin. The exact location in the Orient was not always clear. In the case of transmigration, it might seem that Indian philosophy provided a clue. The Indian poems in *The Wanderings of Oisin and Other Poems* illustrate Yeats's interest in such ideas. In his verse-drama 'Mosada', from the end of that volume, we find a different type of Orient, for the setting is Spain during the Inquisition, and the oriental is represented by a Moorish girl who practises magic and is condemned unknowingly by the hypocritical monk Ebremar, who had once been her lover. The play is in part an allegory about Irish society, for it dramatises the conflict between an oppressive Catholicism and a form of magic Yeats could associate with his own esoteric interests. Nor is it irrelevant that Yeats was a Protestant, brought up in the established, Anglican Church of Ireland.

But there may be more to say about that particular fact than would at first seem likely. It is, of course, suggestive that members of the Church of Ireland had for long seen themselves as the true heirs of 'the Celtic Church', and had sought to represent the Catholic Church as an alien import. Of more direct relevance might be the fact, outlined by Roy Foster in a brilliant lecture, 'Protestant Magic', that there was a strong tradition of interest in the occult among the educated Protestant middle class in Ireland. When Yeats joined the Hermetic Order of the Golden Dawn he was joining an order which was avowedly Rosicrucian. That is to say, it traced its doctrines back to the legendary Christian Rosenkreutz, whose name was interpreted symbolically and related to the doctrines themselves: specifically, these were held to revolve around a symbolic union of Rose and Cross. Yeats's own poem, 'To the Rose Upon the Rood of Time', offers a useful illustration of the workings of these doctrines. Here, the Cross (or Rood) is also seen as a tree, in line with St Paul (Galatians 3:13). This tree that is also a cross of torture and death symbolises the contrariety and struggle of earthly existence. Yet out of this very condition blooms what Yeats calls the 'Eternal Beauty' of the Rose. When one looks at the way in which the Golden Dawn sought a synthesis of many esoteric traditions, including the Jewish Kabbalah, one realises that this tree is also the Tree of Life expounded by the Kabbalists. This had two aspects, one of sternness and rigour (related to God's judgement) and one of mildness (related to His mercy). A tree of double aspect is also part of the background to Yeats's 'The Two Trees', although he may also be thinking of another Kabbalistic tradition to the effect that, after the Fall of Man, the tree appears in this world as dead and lifeless. So much on the central images of Rosicrucianism. The connection with Irish Protestantism relates to three facts: the inner, or more elite and thoughtful, grades of Freemasonry tended to espouse Rosicrucian doctrines, as witnessed by the very names of a number of masonic lodges; Freemasonry was a pervasive institution among Irish Protestants, at least from the late eighteenth century; and Catholics were officially forbidden to be Freemasons. This provides another way of understanding Yeats's own particular version of 'Protestant Magic'. It shows the mystery and magic of his own caste vying with and surpassing those of the Catholic Church.

The picture we have unfolded is one of a thinker and poet who draws the disparate areas of his experience into a unity. His indebtedness to English Romantic poetry, especially that of Blake, cannot be separated from his immersion in esoteric doctrines, and that cannot be separated from his conception of Druidism or ancient Celtic tradition. Naturally enough, Druidism is central to his sense of what the Celtic temperament and wisdom actually were. And the recovery of that temperament and that wisdom are an aim at one with his political hopes for Ireland. This drive to unity is present in the imagery of the poems themselves. The symbol of the Rose, for instance, while palpably indebted to the Rosicrucian doctrine, also comprises references to the personification of Ireland as a rose in an anonymous poem, 'Róisín Dubh' ('little dark rose', translated by Mangan as 'My Dark Rosaleen'). There is probably also a reference to the 'Red Branch', emblem of the ancient dynasty of Ulster whose legendary history is recounted in the ancient sagas and tales. Yeats takes the trouble to ensure that his readers are left in no doubt about the unity of his aims or his belief in the efficacity of that unity. In the 'Apologia' he informs his audience that his interest in magic and the esoteric, so far from being separate from the aim of cultural nationalism, offers a means of reviving the spirit of ancient Ireland. Yeats, like other nineteenth-century Celticists, thought that the marginalisation of the Celts by modern industrial society meant that they had remained nearer to the ancient sources of wisdom. They might help to save humanity from the deadening effects of modernity in a new age, an age of spiritual rebirth which would dawn in the twentieth century. Ideas such as this give a particular content to the undoubted *fin-de-siècle* quality of *The Wind Among the Reeds* (1899), a work which seems conscious of its date of publication. If the Celts were to assist in the renewal of modern Europe, the liberation of Ireland from domination by the world's greatest imperial and industrial power might be a decisive moment in that renewal. In 'The Valley of the Black Pig', from *The Wind Among the Reeds*, Yeats foresees an apocalyptic battle in which Ireland will confront her foes.

Yet the tone of *The Wind Among the Reeds* is anything but triumphant. Many poems are marked by the melancholy of unsatisfied love. Some of them border on depression. Ireland may need to be renewed, but so does the poet, and for this to happen he needs to find a true marriage, such as Aengus envisages for himself – but has not found, being 'old with wandering'. If it is a question of finding the incipient modernism in early Yeats, nowhere is there a more apt example than this identification of sexual and social renewal. This is indeed a Yeats who prefigures Pound, Lawrence, H.D., and the early work of Eliot and Auden. But by what might seem a paradox at first glance, we need to understand fully the writings of the early Yeats. To do this, we need to go back to the poems as they were first encountered by a wide readership. Only in this way can we gauge the true extent of Yeats's immersion in Celticism and the matter of Ireland – for these were the things that became obscured in later collections – and connect them to his other, more evident themes. It is with this thought in mind that this edition seeks to provide the reader with a better idea of the earliest Yeats.

A Note on the Text

This is a first-version edition of Yeats's early poetry, in the sense that it reproduces the poems that appeared in the first three collections of his own poetry. The volumes are *The Wanderings of Oisin and Other Poems* (London: Kegan Paul & Co., 1889); *The Countess Kathleen and Various Legends and Lyrics* (London: Fisher Unwin, 1892); and *The Wind Among the Reeds* (London: Elkin Mathews, 1899). From the contents of these volumes, however, it does not reproduce the text of *The Countess Kathleen*, in line with the persistent tendency among Yeats and his editors and readers to treat this as essentially a dramatic work. Nor does this edition reproduce the texts in *Poems* (London: T. Fisher Unwin, 1895), since that is substantially a revision and reordering of poems to be found in *The Wanderings* and *Legends and Lyrics*. Readers should bear these facts in mind when interpreting the statement that the current edition provides the first versions of Yeats's early poems.

Where (as is usually the case) a poem exists in multiple versions, there are arguments for making many or all of these versions available, in one edition or another. One learns different things about the poet from the different versions, and one also learns about the different publics that were reading them, and the different contexts in which they appeared. On the other hand, there is no ideal version. Abiding by the final version, as if it were vital to find the poet's final intention, may hinder an understanding of a poet's early work and ideas; while going back to early versions may lead to an ill-considered depreciation of the poet's second thoughts. As regards the versions to be found in the first collections of a poet's own work, one needs to remember the fundamental point that these are not the first versions in an absolute sense. At the very least, a poem will exist in one or more manuscripts (probably different from each other, as well) before it is even published in book form. But it may also have been circulated by hand in a fair copy, and have appeared in a journal or in an anthology, or in a selection of other writings by the author. Many of the poems in this volume had a life of this kind before they entered the covers of one of these collections. The argument for reproducing the texts to be found in these collections is that they represent the earliest form in which a very large number of readers encountered these poems. Some of these poems were discarded, never to appear again in Yeats's subsequent collections. It is instructive to become acquainted with them. The verse-drama 'Mosada', for instance, enhances our understanding of Yeats's use of oriental imagery by making very clear the way in which it could be used in an allegorical representation of Irish realities. There are a number of poems about 'fairies' – for example, 'A Lover's Quarrel among the Fairies', 'The Priest and the Fairy' – in *The Wanderings of Oisin and Other Poems*, which are subsequently discarded. These suggest a far more conventional nineteenth-century context than one might have imagined for the development of Yeats's lifelong interest in those uncanny beings, the Sidhe ('fairies') of Irish mythology and folklore. The wording of some of Yeats's best-known poems is sometimes markedly different from the established versions, as is the case with 'Apologia Addressed to Ireland in the Coming Days', which will be more familiar to readers as 'To Ireland in the Coming Times'. In context, the original title can be seen to offer a subtly revolutionary hint which gives more point and urgency to the political aspects of the poem. And the titles of many poems in *The Wind Among the Reeds* contain the names of Gaelic personages from mythology and folklore, instead of the pronoun 'he' familiar from later collections: thus, instead of 'He Wishes for the Cloths of Heaven', we find here 'Aedh Wishes for the Cloths of Heaven'. One gains a heightened sense of the importance to Yeats in the nineties of rediscovering and representing Gaelic tradition.

Bibliography

Texts used for this edition
The Wanderings of Oisin and Other Poems. London: Kegan Paul & Co., 1889.
The Countess Kathleen and Various Legends and Lyrics. London: Fisher Unwin, 1892.
The Wind Among the Reeds. London: Elkin Mathews, 1899.

Scholarly editions of the manuscript materials
Bornstein, George, ed. *The Early Poetry*, Vol. I: Mosada *and* The Island of Statues: *Manuscript Materials*. Ithaca, NY: Cornell University Press, 1986.
Bornstein, George, ed. *The Early Poetry*, Vol. II: The Wanderings of Oisin *and Other Early Poems to 1895*. Ithaca, NY: Cornell University Press, 1994.
Holdsworth, Carolyn, ed. *W.B. Yeats: The Wind Among the Reeds: Manuscript Materials*. Ithaca, NY: Cornell University Press, 1993.

Other relevant scholarly editions
Allt, Peter and Russel K. Alspach, eds. *The Variorum Edition of the Poems of W.B. Yeats*. 2nd edn. New York: Macmillan, 1966.
Bornstein, George and Richard J. Finneran, eds. *The Collected Works of W.B. Yeats*, Vol. IV: *Early Essays*. New York: Scribner, 2007.
Yeats, W.B. *Writings on Irish Folklore, Legend and Myth*. Ed. Robert Welch. Harmondsworth: Penguin, 1993.

Critical and scholarly works
Bloom, Harold. *Yeats*. New York: Oxford University Press, 1970.
Brown, Terence. *The Life of W.B. Yeats: A Critical Biography*. 2nd edn. Oxford: Blackwell, 2001.
Chaudhry, Yug Mohit. *Yeats, the Irish Literary Revival and the Politics of Print*. Cork: Cork University Press, 2001.
Foster, R.F. 'Protestant Magic: W.B. Yeats and the Spell of Irish

History.' *Paddy and Mr Punch: Connections in Irish and English History*. Harmondsworth: Penguin, 1993. 212–32.

Foster, R.F. *W.B. Yeats: A Life*. 2 vols. Oxford: Oxford University Press, 1997–2003. Vol. 1: *The Apprentice Mage*, 1997.

Grene, Nicholas. *Yeats's Poetic Codes*. Oxford: Oxford University Press, 2008.

Grossman, Allen R. *Poetic Knowledge in the Early Yeats: A Study of The Wind Among the Reeds*. Charlottesville: University Press of Virginia, 1969.

Harper, George Mills. *Yeats's Golden Dawn*. London: Macmillan, 1974.

Kermode, Frank. *Romantic Image*. London: Routledge and Kegan Paul, 1957.

Kinahan, Frank. *Yeats, Folklore, and Occultism: Contexts of the Early Work and Thought*. London: Unwin Hyman, 1988.

Larrissy, Edward. *Yeats the Poet: The Measures of Difference*. Hemel Hempstead: Harvester, 1994.

Larrissy, Edward. *Blake and Modern Literature*. Basingstoke: Palgrave Macmillan, 2006.

Lennon, Joseph. 'W.B. Yeats's Celtic Orient.' *Irish Orientalism: A Literary and Intellectual History*. Syracuse, NY: Syracuse University Press, 2004. 247–89.

Matthews, Steven. *Yeats as Precursor: Readings in Irish, British and American Poetry*. Basingstoke: Palgrave Macmillan, 2000.

Pierce, David. *Yeats's Worlds: Ireland, England and the Poetic Imagination*. New Haven and London: Yale University Press, 1995.

Putzel, Steven D. *Reconstructing Yeats: The Secret Rose and The Wind Among the Reeds*. Dublin: Gill and Macmillan, 1986.

Welch, Robert. *Irish Poetry from Moore to Yeats*. Gerrards Cross: Colin Smythe, 1980.

THE WANDERINGS OF OISIN
AND OTHER POEMS
(1889)

The Wanderings of Oisin
and
How a Demon Trapped Him

Part I
The Island of the Living

PATRICK

Oisin, tell me the famous story
Why thou outlivest, blind and hoary,
The bad old days. Thou wert, men sing,
Trapped of an amorous demon thing.

OISIN

'Tis sad remembering, sick with years,
The swift innumerable spears,
The long-haired warriors, the spread feast;
And love, in the hours when youth has ceased:
Yet will I make all plain for thee.
We rode in sorrow, with strong hounds three,
Bran, Sgeolan, and Lomair,
On a morning misty and mild and fair.
The mist-drops hung on the fragrant trees,
And in the blossoms hung the bees.
We rode in sadness above Lough Laen,
For our best were dead on Gavra's green.
The stag we chased was not more sad,
And yet, of yore, much peace he had
In his own leafy forest house,
Sleek as any granary mouse
Among the fields of waving fern.
We thought on Oscar's pencilled urn.
Than the hornless deer we chased that morn,
A swifter creature never was born,
And Bran, Sgeolan, and Lomair
Were lolling their tongues, and the silken hair
Of our strong steeds was dark with sweat,

When ambling down the vale we met
A maiden, on a slender steed,
Whose careful pastern pressed the sod
As though he held an earthly mead
Scarce worthy of a hoof gold-shod.
For gold his hooves and silk his rein,
And 'tween his ears, above his mane,
A golden crescent lit the plain,
And pearly white his well-groomed hair.
His mistress was more mild and fair
Than doves that moaned round Eman's hall
Among the leaves of the laurel wall,
And feared always the bow-string's twanging.
Her eyes were soft as dewdrops hanging
Upon the grass-blades' bending tips,
And like a sunset were her lips,
A stormy sunset o'er doomed ships.
Her hair was of a citron tincture,
And gathered in a silver cincture;
Down to her feet white vesture flowed
And with the woven crimson glowed
Of many a figured creature strange,
And birds that on the seven seas range.
For brooch 'twas bound with a bright sea-shell,
And wavered like a summer rill,
As her soft bosom rose and fell.

PATRICK
Oisin, thou art half heathen still!

OISIN
'Why, as ye ride, droops low each head?
Why do ye sound no horn?' she said.
'For hunting heroes should be glad.
The stag ye chase is not more sad,
And yet, of yore, much peace he had,
Sleek as any granary mouse,
In his own leafy forest house,
Among the waving fields of fern.'

'We think on Oscar's pencilled urn,
And those on Gavra lying low,
Where round and round the ravens go.
Now, pleasant maiden, tell to me
Thy name, thy kin, and thy country,'
Cried Fin; and cried she, 'Men of fame,
My home is far from where the tide
Washes the shores where ye abide,
Ye worn deed-doers, and my name
Is Niam, daughter of the King
Of the Young.'
          'Young maiden, what may bring
Thy wandering steps across the sea?
Is thy companion gone from thee?'
Clear fluted then that goblin rare –
'Not so, great king; for I have ne'er
Been spoken of with any man.
For love of Oisin my feet ran
Across the glossy sea.'
          'Oh, wild
Young princess, why wert thou beguiled
Of Oisin, the young man, my son?
Of princes there is many a one.'
'Good reason have I for my love,'
She said; 'for he is fair above
All men, and stronger of his hands,
And drops of honey are his words,
And glorious as Asian birds
At evening in their rainless lands.
Full many bowing kings besought me,
And many princes of high name.
I ne'er loved any till song brought me
To peak and pine o'er Oisin's fame.'
There was, oh Patrick, by thy head,
No limb of me that was not fallen
In love. I cried, 'Thee will I wed,
Young Niam, and thou shalt be callen
Beloved in a thousand songs.
Before thy feet shall kneel down all

My captives, bound in leathern thongs,
And praise thee in my western hall.'
'Oisin, thou must away with me
To my own kingdom in the sea –
Away, away with me,' she cried,
'To shores by the wash of the tremulous tide,
Where the voice of change is the voice of a tune,
In the poppy-hung house of the twilight fluted;
To shores where dying has never been known,
And the flushes of first love never have flown;
And a hundred steeds, tumultuous-footed,
There shalt thou have, and a hundred hounds
That spring five paces in their bounds,
No mightier creatures bay at the moon;
And a hundred robes of the softest silk,
And a hundred calves, and a hundred sheep
Whose long wool whiter than sea-froth flows;
And a hundred swords and a hundred bows;
And honey, and oil, and wine, and milk,
And always never-anxious sleep;
And a hundred maidens wise and young,
And sweeter of voice than the pleasant birds,
And swifter than the salmon herds;
And a hundred youths, whose limbs are strung
In a vigour more than mortal measure,
And floating-haired and proud in strife;
And thou shalt know the immortals' leisure,
And I be with thee as thy wife.'

We rode beyond the furze and heather,
And stood beside the sea together;
Then sighed she softly, 'Late! 'tis late!
Mount my white steed, for the fairy state
Lies far.' I mounted, and she bound me
In triumph with her arms around me,
And, whispering to herself, enwound me;
And when the white steed felt my weight,
He shook himself for travelling,
And neighed three times.

When, wondering
Near by, the Fenians saw, and knew
That I would go with her, they grew
Mournful, and gathered on the sands;
They wept, and raised lamenting hands.
When I had stooped and tenderly
Had kissed my father, long-armed Fin,
And the Fenians all had wept with me,
We rode across the oily sea,
For the sparkling hooves they sank not in;
And far behind us, slowly round
The Fenians on the human ground
Closed in the misty air profound.
In what far kingdom do ye go,
Ah, Fenians, with the shield and bow?
Or are ye phantoms white as snow,
Whose lips had life's most prosperous glow,
Oh ye with whom, in sloping valleys
And down the dewy forest alleys,
I chased with hounds the flying deer,
With whom I hurled the hurrying spear,
And heard the foeman's bucklers rattle,
And broke the heaving ranks of battle?
And, Bran, Sgeolan, and Lomair,
Where are ye with your long rough hair?
Ye go not where the red deer feeds,
Nor tear the foemen from their steeds.

PATRICK

Bard Oisin, boast not of thy deeds
Nor thy companions. Let them rest,
The Fenians. Let their deer-hounds sleep.
Tell on, nor bow thy heathen crest
In brooding memory, nor weep.

OISIN

On, on, we galloped o'er the sea.
I knew not if days passed or hours,
For fairy songs continually

Sang Niam, and their dewy showers
Of pensive laughter – unhuman sound –
Lulled weariness; and closely round
My human sadness fay arms wound.
On, on! and now a hornless deer
Passed by us, chased of a phantom hound
All pearly white, save one red ear;
And now a maid, on a swift brown steed
Whose hooves the tops of the surges grazed,
Hurried away, and over her raised
An apple of gold in her tossing hand;
And following her at a headlong speed
Was a beautiful youth from an unknown land.
'Who are the riding ones?' I said.
'Fret not with speech the phantoms dread,'
Said Niam, as she laid the tip
Of one long finger on my lip.
Now in the sea the sun's rim sank,
The clouds arrayed them rank on rank
In silence round his crimson ball.
The floor of Eman's dancing hall
Was not more level than the sea,
As, full of loving phantasy,
We rode on murmuring. Many a shell
That in immortal silence sleeps
And dreams of her own melting hues,
Her golds, her azures, and her blues,
Pierced with soft light the shallowing deeps,
When round us suddenly there came
A far vague sound of feathery choirs.
It seemed to fall from the very flame
Of the great round sun, from his central fires.
The steed towards the music raced,
Neighing along the lifeless waste;
And, as the sun sank ever lower,
Like sooty fingers many a tree
Rose ever from the sea's warm floor,
And they were trembling ceaselessly,
As though they all were beating time

Upon the centre of the sun
To the music of the golden rhyme
Sung of the birds. Our toil was done;
We cantered to the shore, and knew
The reason of the trembling trees,
For round each branch the song-birds flew,
Or clung as close as swarms of bees,
While round the shore a million stood
Like drops of frozen rainbow light,
And pondered in a soft vain mood
On their own selves in the waters white,
And murmured snatches of delight;
And on the shores were many boats
With bending sterns and bending bows,
And carven figures on their prows
Of bitterns and fish-eating stoats,
And swans with their exultant throats.
Among them 'lighting from our steed,
Maid Niam from a little trump
Blew one long note. From over reed
And river, fern and flowery clump,
Ere long an answering whisper flew,
A whisper of impetuous feet
Among the woodland grasses sweet,
And ever nearer, nearer grew;
And from the woods there rushed a band
Of youths and maidens hand in hand,
And singing, singing all together.
Their brows were white as fragrant milk,
Their robes were all of yellow silk,
Trimmed round with many a crimson feather;
And when they saw my earthly dress,
They fingered it and gazed at me,
And laughed like murmurs of the sea.
But Niam, with a sad distress,
Bid them away and hold their peace;
And when they heard her voice, they ran
And knelt them, every maid and man,
And kissed, as they would never cease,

Her fingers and her garments' hem.
Now in the woods, away with them
Went we to find their prince's hall —
On in the woods, away with them,
Where white dewdrops in millions fall;
On in the woods, away with them,
Where tangling creepers every hour
Blossom in some new crimson flower;
On in the woods, away with them,
Where trees made sudden cavern-glooms
By roots that joined above our plumes —
On in the woods, away with them!
And once a sudden laughter sprang
From all their lips, and once they sang
Together, while the dark woods rang,
And rose from all their distant parts,
From bees among their honey marts,
A rumour of delighted hearts.
And while they sang, a singer laid
A harp of silver in my hands,
And bade me sing of earthly lands;
And when I sang of human joy
They hushed them, every man and maid.
Oh, Patrick, by thy beard, they wept,
And one came close, a tearful boy.
'A sadder creature never stept
Than this strange bard,' he cried, and caught
The harp away. A dolorous pool
Lay 'neath us; of its hollow cool
No creature had familiar thought
Save deer towards noon that water sought.
Therein the silver harp he hurled,
And each one said, with a long, long sigh,
'The saddest harp in all the world!'

And now still sad our troop drew nigh
A firwood house, all covered over
With antlers and the shaggy skin
Of many a slaughtered forest rover.

We passed the portals, and within,
One hand beneath his beardless chin,
There was a wondrous young man sitting.
Within his other hand were flitting
Around a sceptre of all lights,
Wild flames of red and creamy whites,
Wild flames of red and gold and blue;
And nigh unto him each one drew,
And kissed the sceptre with hot lips,
And touched it with his finger-tips.

With a clear voice the young man cried,
"Tis joy makes swim the sappy tide,
And "Waken, courtiers of the morn!"
Cries to the sluggard seeds of corn,
And stirs the young kid's budding horn,
And makes the infant ferns unwrap,
And for the peewit paints his cap.
For joy the little planets run
Round us, and rolls the unwieldy sun.
If joy were nowhere on the earth
There were an end of change and birth;
The universe herself would die,
And in some urn funereal lie
Folded like a frozen fly.

'The soul is a drop of joy afar.
In other years from some old star
It fell, or from the twisted moon
Dripped on the earth; but soon, ah! soon,
To all things cried, "I am a slave!
Trickling along the earth, I rave;
In pinching ways I toil and turn."
But, warrior, here there is no law;
The soul is free, and finds no flaw,
Nor sorrow with her osprey claw.
Then, warrior, why so sad and stern,
For joy is God and God is joy?'

Among the ringing halls a shout
Arose from every maid and boy,
And through the doors, a rustling rout,
Swept on the dance's linkèd flow,
In every brain a wizard glow.
Beside the sea, where, hushed and slow,
The murmuring birds in solemn pomp
Passed a-tiptoe up and down
In a long and shadowy row,
We hushed the singing and the romp,
And, gathering on our brows a frown,
Whispered to the sea whose flow
Eat away the sloping sod,
'God is joy and joy is God.
Everything that's sad is wicked —
Everything that fears to-morrow
Or the wild grey osprey sorrow.'

Then onward in the winding thicket
We danced to where within the gloom
Hung, like meteors of red light,
Damask roses in the night,
And sang we lightly to each bloom
As we kissed each rose's head;
Sang we softly in the dance,
With a swift and friendly glance —
Sang we softly, 'On the dead,
Fall the leaves of other roses,
On the dead the earth encloses.
Never, never on our graves,
Heaved beside the glimmering waves,
Shall fall the leaves of damask roses;
For change and death they come not near us,
And all listless hours fear us,
And we never fear the morrow
Or the wild grey osprey sorrow.'

Then on among the windless woods,
The ever summered solitudes,

The many-coloured dancers rushed,
Till on the central hill we hushed
Once more the dance's linkèd flow,
And, gathered in a panting band,
Flung on high each waving hand,
And sang unto the starry broods.
In our raised eyes there flashed a glow
Of milky brightness to and fro,
As thus our song arose: 'Ye stars,
Across your wandering ruby cars
Shake the loose reins! Ye slaves of God,
He rules you with an iron rod,
He holds you with an iron bond,
Each one woven to the other,
Each one woven to his brother,
Like bubbles in a frozen pond.
But we, oh rolling stars, are free.
The ever-winding wakeful sea,
That hides us from all human spying,
Is not so free, so free, so free.
Our hands have known no wearying tool,
Our lives have known no law nor rule;
Afar from where the years are flying
O'er men who sleep, and wake, and die,
And peak and pine we know not why,
We only know that we were glad
Aforetime, and shall not grow sad
Or tired on any dawning morrow,
Nor ever change or feel the clutches
Of grievous Time on his old crutches,
Or fear the wild grey osprey sorrow.'

Oh, Patrick, on that woody shore
A hundred years I chased the boar,
And slew the badger and the deer,
And flung the joyous hunting-spear!
Oh, Patrick, there a hundred seasons
I loved and sang, and in long wassails
I laughed at time's unnumbered treasons,

And twice a hundred were the vassals
That followed my keen hunting-call –
For love they followed one and all!
Oh, Patrick, there a hundred years,
At evening, on the glimmering sands,
These now o'erworn and withered hands,
Beside the piled-up hunting-spears,
Wrestled among the island bands!
Oh, Patrick, for a hundred years
We went a-fishing in long boats
With bending sterns and bending bows,
And carven figures on their prows
Of bitterns and fish-eating stoats!
Oh, Patrick, for a hundred years
The gentle Niam was my wife!
And now have fallen on my life
Two things that 'fore all else I hate,
Fasting and prayers.

PATRICK
Tell on.

OISIN
                                    Ay, ay!
For these were ancient Oisin's fate,
Loosed long ago from heaven's gate,
For his last days to lie in wait.
When once beside the shore I stood,
A sea-worn waif came floating by.
I drew it forth; the staff of wood,
It was of some dead warrior's lance.
I turned it in my hands; the stains
Of war were on it, and I wept,
Remembering how along the plains,
Equal to good or evil chance
In war, the noble Fenians stept.
Then softly to me Niam came,
And caught my hands and spake no word,
Save only many times my name,

In murmurs like a frighted bird.
We passed in silence o'er the mead,
By woods of moss, by lawns of clover,
And once more saddled the white steed,
For well we knew the old was over,
And rode and stood beside the shore.
I heard one say, 'Within his eyes
The human sadness dawns once more;'
I saw not who; 'neath other skies
My dreams were living. Now the hoof
Pressed on the ever-trembling roof
Of murmuring ocean, and behind us
The isle loomed largely in the light
Of languid evening that entwined us.
The fairies moved among the fountains,
The rivers, and the wood's old night.
Some danced like shadows on the mountains;
And others sat them by the sea,
Each forehead, like an obscure star,
Bent low above each hookèd knee,
And sang, and with a dreamy gaze
Watched the old sun that in sea-ways
Half slumbered with his saffron blaze;
And as they sang, the painted birds
Beat time with their bright wings and feet.
Like drops of honey came their words
Thus on the waters, far and sweet,
And fainter than a young lamb's bleat.

'Swift are the years of a warrior's pride;
    It passeth away, and is heard of no longer.
In honour soon by his master's side
    Sits a younger and a stronger.
His toothless hound at his nerveless feet,
    The warrior dreams in an aged leisure
Of the things that his heart still knows were sweet –
    Of war, and the chase, and hunting, and pleasure;
And blows on his hands in the fire's warm blaze;
    In the house of his friend, of his kin, of his brother,

He hath over lingered his welcome; the days,
   Grown desolate, whisper and sigh to each other.

'But never with us where the wild fowl chases
   His shadow along in the evening blaze,
Will the softness of youth be gone from our faces,
   Or love's first tenderness die in our gaze.

'A storm of birds in the Asian trees
   Like tulips in the air a-winging,
And the gentle waves of the summer seas
   That raise their heads and wander singing,
By age's weariness are slain,
   And the long grey grasses, whose tenderest touches
Stroked the young winds as they rolled on the plain,
   The osprey of sorrow goes after and clutches,
And they cease with a sigh of "Unjust! unjust!"
   And "A weariness soon is my speed," says the mouse,
And the kingfisher turns to a ball of dust,
   And the roof falls in of his tunnelled house.

'But never the years in the isle's soft places
   Will scatter in ruin the least of our days,
Or the softness of youth be gone from our faces,
   Or love's first tenderness die in our gaze.

'Old grows the hare as she plays in the sun,
   And gazes around her with eyes of brightness;
Ere half the swift things that she dreamt on were done,
   She limps along in an aged whiteness.
And even the sun, the day castle's warder,
   That scares with his bustle the delicate night,
And shakes o'er the width of the sea-world border
   The odorous weight of his curls of light,
Like a bride bending over her mirror adorning,
   May sleep in the end with the whole of his fate done,
And the stars shall arise and say in the morning,
   As they gaze at each other, "Oh, where is that great one?"

'But never the years in our isle's soft places
  Shall blow into ruin our musical days,
Or the softness of youth be gone from our faces,
  Or love's first tenderness die in our gaze.'

The singing melted in the night;
  The isle was over now and gone;
The mist closed round us; pearly light
  On horse and sea and saddle shone.

Part II
The Island of Victories

Now, man of crosiers, phantoms drew around
Once more – the youth and lady, deer and hound;
Half lost in vapour, shadows called our names,
And then away, away like spiral flames.
'These forms?' 'Vex not with speech the phantoms dread.'
And now sang Niam, swaying her bright head
And her bright body – now of fay and man;
Things done ere God first was or my old line began;
Wars shadowy, vast, exultant; fairy kings
Wedding the queens of earthly lands with rings
Of sea-sprung pearl, and queens of fairy lands
Taking the mortal warriors by the hands;
How such a warrior never turned his gaze
On the old sorrows of his human days.
They love and kiss in islands far away,
Rolled round with music of the sighing spray,
Those warriors of a long-forgotten day,
Happy as children with unwithering lips,
Unlanguid as the birds, in proud companionships;
They walk on shores unseen of oaring galleys,
Or wrestle with their peers in dewy valleys.
So sang young Niam, swaying her bright head,
No longer glad as on that morning, sped
To join his brothers in the home of years

A hundred seasons; for a sound of tears
Floated in all her singing. Half entranced
I lay, as over sea the light hooves glanced
Flashing – I know not were it hours or days,
Yet dimly deem I that the morning rays
Shone many times among the glimmering flowers
In Niam's hair – when rose a world of towers
And blackness in the dark. The sea rolled round,
Crazed with its own interminable sound,
And when the white steed saw what blackness gleamed,
He shivering paused, and raised his head and screamed.
But Niam with her hands caressed his ears,
And called him sweetest names and soothed his fears.
Nearer the castle came we. A vast tide,
Whitening the surge afar, fan-formed and wide,
Sprang from a gateway walled around with black
Basaltic pillars marred with hew and hack
By mace and spear and sword of sea-gods, nails
Of some forgotten fiend. Now none assails
That old, sea-weedy, squared, three hundred feet
Uplifted gateway. With the flashing beat
Of Danaan hooves we urged our way between
Two walls, a roof, a flood: there trembling green
Of surging phosphorus alone gave light.
At last the moon and stars shone, and a flight
Of many thousand steps. Sat either side,
Fog-dripping, pedestalled above the tide,
Huge forms of stone; between the lids of one
The imaged meteors had shone and run,
And had disported in the eyes still jet
For centuries, and stars had dawned and set.
He seemed the watcher for a sign. The other
Stretched his long arm to where, a misty smother,
The stream churned, churned, and churned. His lips were rolled apart,
As though unto his never slumbering heart
He told of every froth-drop hissing, flying.
We mounted on the stair, the white steed tying,
To one vast foot, froth-splashed, with curved toes lying
Half in the unvesselled sea.

THE FIRST YEATS

We'd mounted far;
So much remained that on the evening star
I thought the end had rested, when these words
From high above, like feathers of young birds
That fan the pulses of delighted air,
Came swimming sadly down the mighty stair.

'My brothers and my sisters live and thrive,
And chase the wild bee homeward to his hive
    Afar in ancient Eri,
By lakes and meadow lands and lawns afar,
Where goes to gaze the restless-footed star
    Of twilight when he's weary.

'They murmur like young partridge in the morn,
When they awake upspringing; with loud horn
    They chase at noon the deer.
When the earliest dew-washed star from eve hath leant,
Then muse they on the household wool intent,
    Or carve a dreadful spear.

'Oh, sigh, awake and go you forth for me;
Flutter along the froth-lips of the sea,
    And go you close to them.
From sleeper unto sleeper murmur you.
If they still slumber, touch their eyelids blue,
    And shake their coverlet's hem,

'And tell them how I weep, until they weep;
Then, mounted on a heron, o'er the deep
    Return when you are weary,
And tell me how my kindred's tears are welling,
And one whom you will go to without telling,
    Say how he weeps in Eri.'

Crashed on the stones, upon the glimmering stones,
Our tread, as rose and fell the liquid tones
Of knitted music. Oft the fond repining
Flowed on anew, and oft, anew declining,

Sobbed into silence. We had mounted feet
Full many more, when peered a maiden sweet
Down on us with her eyes like funeral tapers.
Her face seemed fashioned all of moonlit vapours,
So pale! And sounds of wonder her lips uttered,
As like a ruddy moth they waved and fluttered.
To eagles twain that, full of ancient pride,
Stood lonely, with dim eyeballs on each side,
With chain sea-rotted, round her middle tied,
Chained was she. On their wings the hundredth year
Scarce left a whitening feather, grey and sere;
And through their eyes no light of moon or day
Smote on their brains that dwelt remembering aye.
And thus, my late-lost Niam, didst thou say:
'I bring thee a deliverer from far away,
Oh maiden.'
       'Are ye spirits of the sea,
Or of the flaked clouds?'
         'Not so, for we
Come from the Isle of the Living.'
         'Then get ye
Once more unto your flowers, for none may fight,
With hope, mine enemy. As he by night
Goes dropping from his eyes a languid light,
The demons of the wilds and winds for fright
Jabber and scream. Yet he, for all his bold
And flowing strength, with age is subtle-souled.
None may beguile him, and his passions cold
Long while, are whips of steel.'
         'Is he so dread?'
Said Niam.
       'Ay, and huge. When ye have led
A jubilant life among the leaves, return,
Young warrior.'
       'Nay,' I answered; 'my hands burn
For battle.'
       'Fly ye from a thing so dread.
It brings no shame upon a human head
To fly a spirit,' Niam weeping said.

Though from beseeching they desisted not,
They stirred my spacious soul in me no jot –
My soul, once glory of its ancient line,
Now old and mouselike. For an answering sign
I burst the chain. Still earless, nerveless, blind,
Rolled in the things of the unhuman mind,
Wrapt round in some dim memory, it seemed –
Still earless, nerveless, blind, the eagles dreamed.
And up the stair we toiled to a high door,
Wherethrough a hundred horsemen on the floor
Basaltic, might have paced. We held our way
And stood within the hall. A misty ray
Clothing him round, I saw a seagull float
Drifting on high, and with a straining throat
Shouted and hailed him. Still he hung content,
For never mortal cry so far hath sent.
Not e'en thy God could have thrown down that hall;
Stabling His unloosed lightnings in their stall,
He had gone whispering forth with cumbered heart,
As though His hour were on Him. To the part
Most distant strode we. On the floor lay slime,
Greenish and slippery. Time after time
The netted marks of crawling scales sea-sprung
We saw, some new, some printed when the place was young,
Grey in the midst like a small rivulet's flow,
The captives' footsteps written to and fro;
And where our footfall 'lighted last there came
A momentary glimmer of vague phosphorous flame.
Feebler and feebler shone the misty glare.
Who brought us found a torch, and, with its flare
Making a world about her, passed from sight
Awhile, and came again, a second light
Burning between her fingers, and in mine
Laid it and sighed – a sword whose wizard shine
Not loaded centuries might vapour. Ran
Deep sunken on the blade's length, 'Mananan!'
Sea-god, that once, to give his slaves content,
Sprang dripping, and, with captive demons sent
From the whole seven seas, those towers set

Rooted in foam and clouds. There mightier masters met
To rule more mighty men, and to the world
Shouted. With fire of hair about her swirled,
The stranger watched the sword; but Niam far,
Scared of its glittering like a meteor star,
Stood timidly. Lest they should see some sight
Of fear, I bade them go; and for the fight
Anointing, torch jammed down between the flags,
Waited. Above, in endless carven jags,
Lifted the dome, where face in carven face
Melted and flowed; and in the self-same place
Hour after hour I waited, and the dome
Windowless, pillarless, multitudinous home
Of faces, watched me, and the leisured gaze
Was loaded with the memory of days
Buried and mighty. Thence I journeyed not
Till the far doorway grew a burning blot
Of misty dawn; when, circling round the hall,
I found a door deep-sunken in the wall,
The least of doors; beyond the door a plain,
Dusky and herbless, where a bubbling strain
Rose from a little runnel on whose edge
A dusk demon, dry as a withered sedge,
Swayed, crooning to himself an unknown tongue.
In a sad revelry he sang and swung,
Bacchant and mournful, passing to and fro
His hand along the runnel's side, as though
The flowers still grew there. Moved beyond him the sea's waste;
Shaking and waving vapours vapours chased;
Dawn passioned; fed with a faint green light,
Like drifts of laurel leaves, immovable and bright
Hung the frail loftier cloudlets. Turned he slow –
A demon's leisure. Eyes first white as snow,
Kingfisher colour grew with rage. He rose
Barking. Along the herbless plain, with blows
Mingling of sword and war-axe, while the day
Gave to the noon, and noon to eve gave way,
We trampled to and fro. When his mind knew

The dead god's sword, to many forms he grew,
Evading, turning; once did I hew and hew
A fir tree roaring in its leafless top,
Once held between my arms, with livid chop
And sunken shape, a nine days' corpse sea-dashed –
Forms without number! When the live west flashed
With surge of plumy fire, lounging I drave
Through heart and demon spine, and in the wave
Cast the loose bulk, lest Niam fear him dead;
And they who to a far-off place had fled,
Hoping and fearing, brought me wine and bread.
The seashine on our faces, we our way
Held to the towers with boasting songs and gay.
With witchery and unguents from the flowers
That lackey the worn moon in midnight hours,
Feeding white moths around some Eastern shrine,
They healed my wounds; and on the skin supine
Of wolves, of boreal bears, we quaffed the wine
Brewed of the sea-gods, from huge cups that lay
Upon the lips of sea-gods in their day,
And on the skins of wolves and bears we slept;
And when the sun in all his flagrant saffron stept,
Rolling his wheel, we sang beside the deep
The spacious loves, the anger without sleep
Of ancient warriors, the labours of the strong.
Patrick, before thy craft dies each old song.
Liar and flatterer of the weak, in what strange clime
Shall they turn wroth or pluck the wings of Time?
Hopeless for ever, they alone shall seek
And never find, though ye in music speak.
Ay, Oisin knows, for he is of the weak,
Blind and nigh deaf, with withered arms he lies
Upon the anvil of the world.

PATRICK
                    The skies
Darken; Heaven is angry. Cease!

OISIN
                    Unto my mind,

Old and remembering, what avails the wind
And lightning flash for ever?

PATRICK

       Cease and hear.
God shakes the world with restless hands. More near
The darkness comes. A cloud hangs overhead –
A hush. Ah, me! it hangs to strike us dead.

A song of MONKS *without.*

'Each one a horsehair shirt hath on,
And many *Pater nosters* said since dawn.
Trembling, on the flags we fall,
Fearful of the thunder-ball,
Yet do with us whate'er thou wilt,
For great our error, great our guilt.'

OISIN

Saint, dost thou weep? I hear amid the thunder
The horses of the Fenians – tearing asunder
Of armour – laughter and cries – the armies' shock.
'Tis over; far with memory I sway and rock.
Ah, cease, thou mournful, laughing Fenian horn!

Three days we feasted, when on the fourth morn
I found, foam-oozy on the vasty stair,
Hung round with slime, and whispering in his hair,
That demon dull and unsubduable,
And we once more unto our fighting fell.
And in the eve I threw him in the surge,
To lie there 'till the fourth day saw emerge
His healèd shape; and for a hundred years
So warred, so feasted we. No dreams, no fears,
No languor, no fatigue; an endless feast,
An endless war.
      The hundredth year had ceased.
I stood upon the stair; the surges bore
A beech bough to me, and my heart grew sore,

Remembering how I paced in days gone o'er,
At Eman, 'neath the beech trees, on each side,
Fin, Conan, Oscar, many more, the tide
Of planets watching, watching the race of hares
Leap in the meadow. On the misty stairs,
Immediate, mournful, white with sudden cares,
Holding that horse long seen not, Niam stood.
With no returning glance, in wordless mood
I mounted, and we rode across the lone
And drifting greyness. Came this monotone
Rising and falling, mixed inseparably,
Surly and distant, with the winds and sea: —

'Age after age I feel my soul decay
Like rotted flesh, and stone by stone my hall
Gathers sea-slime and goes the seaward way,
Thundering, and the wide useless waters fray
        My pillars towards their fall.

'Last of my race, three things I rule alone —
My soul, my prey, and this my heapèd pile.
I pace remembering. From my misty throne
I bellow to the winds when storms make moan,
        And trample my dark isle.

'With all in all the world I battle wage.
The strongest of the world, to snatch my prey,
Came to my tower as age dragged after age.
Light is man's love and lighter is man's rage —
        His purpose drifts away.'

It died afar. Grey sleet those towers hid
And thickened all the whirling air. Then did
Lost Niam mourn and say, 'Ah, love, we go
To the Island of Forgetfulness; for lo,
Isles of the Living and of Victories,
Ye have no power.' 'And, Niam, say, of these
Which is the Isle of Youth?' 'None know,' she said,
And on my bosom laid her weeping head.

Part III
The Island of Forgetfulness

Fled foam underneath us, and round us a wandering and milky smoke,
High as the saddle-girth, covering away from our glances the tide;
The deer and the hound, and the lady and youth, from the distance
broke;
The immortal desire of immortals we saw in their faces, and sighed.

I mused on the chase with the Fenians, and Bran, Sgeolan, Lomair,
And never a song sang Niam, and over my fingertips
Came now the sliding of tears and sweeping of mist-cold hair,
And now the warmth of sighs, and after the quiver of lips.

Were we days long or hours long in riding, when rolled in a grisly
peace,
An isle lay level before us, dripping with hazel and oak?
And we stood on a sea's edge we saw not; for whiter than
new-washed fleece
Fled foam underneath us, and round us a wandering and milky smoke.

And we rode on the plains of the sea's edge – the sea's edge barren
and grey,
Grey sands on the green of the grasses and over the dripping trees,
Dripping and doubling landward, as though they would hasten away
Like an army of old men longing for rest from the moan of the seas.

But taller the trees grew and closer, immense in their wrinkling bark;
Dropping – a murmurous dropping – old silence and that one sound;
For no live creatures lived there, no weasels moved in the dark –
Long sighs arose in our spirits, beneath us bubbled the ground.

And the ears of the horse went sinking away in the hollow night,
For, as drift from a sailor slow drowning the gleams of the world
and the sun,
Ceased on our hands and our faces, on hazel and oak leaf, the light,
And the stars were blotted above us, and the whole of the world
was one.

Till the horse gave a whinny; for, cumbrous with stems of the
                                                        hazel and oak,
Of hollies, and hazels, and oak trees, a valley was sloping away
From his hooves in the heavy grasses, with monstrous slumbering folk,
Their mighty and naked and gleaming bodies heaped loose where
                                                        they lay.

More comely than man may make them, inlaid with silver and gold,
Were arrow and shield and war-axe, arrow and spear and blade,
And dew-blanched horns, in whose hollows a child of three years old
Could sleep on a couch of rushes – round and about them laid.

And each of the huge white creatures was huger than fourscore men;
The tops of their ears were feathered, their hands were the claws of
                                                        birds,
And, shaking the plumes of the grasses and the leaves of the mural glen,
The breathing came from those bodies, long-warless, grown whiter
                                                        than curds.

So spacious the wood was above them, that He who has stars for
                                                        His flocks
Could fondle the leaves with His fingers, nor go from His
                                                        dew-cumbered skies;
So long were they sleeping, the owls had builded their nests in
                                                        their locks,
Filling the fibrous dimness with long generations of eyes.

And over the limbs and the valley the slow owls wandered and came,
Now in a place of star-fire, and now in a shadow place wide;
And the chief of the huge white creatures, his knees in the soft
                                                        star-flame,
Lay loose in a place of shadow – we drew the reins by his side.

Golden the nails of his bird-claws, flung loosely along the dim ground;
In one was a branch soft-shining with bells more many than sighs
In the midst of an old man's bosom; owls ruffling and pacing around,
Sidled their bodies against him, filling the shade with their eyes.

And my gaze was thronged with the sleepers – no, neither in
                              household of Can,
In a realm where the handsome are many, or in glamours by
                              demons flung,
Are faces alive with such beauty made known to the salt eye of man,
Yet weary with passions that faded when the sevenfold seas were young;

And I gazed on the bell-branch, sleep's forebear, far sung of the
                              Sennachies.
I saw how those slumberers, grown weary, there camping in grasses
                              deep,
Of wars with the wide world and pacing the shores of the seven seas,
Laid hands on the bell-branch and swayed it, and fed of unhuman
                              sleep.

Snatching the horn of Niam, I blew forth a lingering note;
Came sound from those monstrous sleepers, a sound like the
                              stirring of flies.
He, shaking the folds of his lips and heaving the pillar of his throat,
Watched me with mournful wonder out of the wells of his eyes.

I cried, 'Thou art surely a warrior, forgetting his famous line,
And even the names of his fathers, and even the works of his hands?
A good name is goodly to hear of, and a good name surely is thine.
Worthy's thy questioner, Oisin, he from the Fenian lands.'

Half open his eyes were, and held me, dull with the smoke of their
                              dreams;
His lips moved slowly in answer, no answer out of them came;
Then he swayed in his fingers the bell-branch, slow dropping a
                              sound in faint streams,
Softer than snowflakes in April, and piercing the marrow like flame.

Wrapt in the wave of that music, with weariness more than of earth,
The moil of my centuries filled me; and gone like a sea-covered stone
Were the memories of the whole of my sorrow and the memories
                              of the whole of my mirth,
And a softness came from the starlight and filled me full to the bone.

In the roots of the grasses, the sorrels, I laid my body as low;
Sad Niam came near me, and laid her brows on the midst of my
breast;
And the horse was gone in the distance, and years after years 'gan
their flow;
Square leaves of the ivy moved over us, binding us down to our rest.

And, man of the many white crosiers, a century there I forgot –
How the fetlocks drip blood in the battle, when the fallen on fallen
lie rolled;
How the falconer follows the falcon in the weeds of the heron's plot,
And the names of the demons whose hammers made armour for
Conor the old.

And, man of the many white crosiers, a century there I forgot;
That the spearshaft is made out of ashwood, the shield out of osier
and hide;
How the hammers spring on the anvil, on the spearhead's burning
spot;
How the slow blue-eyed oxen of Fin low sadly at evening tide.

But in dreams, mild man of the crosiers, driving the dust with their
throngs,
Moved round me, of seamen or landsmen, all who are winter tales;
Came by me the kings of the Red Branch with roaring of laughter
and songs,
Or moved as they moved once, love-making or piercing the
tempest with sails.

Came Blanid, Mac Nessa, Cuchulin; came Fergus who feastward
sad slunk,
Cook Barach, the traitor; and warward, the spittle on his beard
never dry,
Came car-borne Balor, as old as a forest, his vast face sunk
Helpless, men lifting the lids of his weary and death-pouring eye.

And by me, in soft red raiment, the Fenians moved in loud streams;
And Grania walking and smiling, sewed with her needle of bone.
So lived I and lived not, so wrought I and wrought not, with
creatures of dreams,
In a long iron sleep, as a fish in the water goes dumb as a stone.

At times our slumber was lightened. When the sun was on silver or
                                              gold;
When brushed with the wings of the owls, in the dimness they
                                      love going by;
When a glow-worm was green on a grass leaf, lured from his lair in
                                        the mould,
Half wakening, we lifted our eyelids, and gazed on the grass with a sigh,

So watched I when, man of the crosiers, at the heel of a century fell,
Weak, in the midst of the meadow, from his miles in the midst of
                                        the air,
A starling – like them that foregathered 'neath a moon waking
                                  white as a shell,
When the Fenians made foray at morning with Bran, Sgeolan, Lomair.

I awoke – the strange horse without summons out of the distance ran,
Thrusting his nose to my shoulder – he knew in his bosom deep
That once more moved in my bosom the ancient sadness of man,
And that I would leave the immortals, their dimness, their dews
                                    dropping sleep.

Oh, hadst thou seen beautiful Niam wail to herself and blanch,
Lord of the crosiers, thou even hadst lifted thy hands and wept;
But, the bird in my fingers, I mounted, mindful only to launch
Forth, piercing the distance – beneath me the hooves impatiently stept.

I cried, 'Oh, Niam! oh, white one! if only a twelve-houred day
I must gaze on the beard of Fin, and move where the old men and
                                    young
In the Fenian's dwellings of wattle lean on the chessboards and play,
Ah, sweet to me now were even bald Conan's slanderous tongue!

'Like me were some galley forsaken far off in Meridian isle,
Remembering its long-oared companions, sails turning to
                                  threadbare rags;
No more to crawl on the seas with long oars mile after mile,
But to be 'mid the shooting of flies and the flowering of rushes and
                                  flags.'

Their motionless eyeballs of spirits grown mild with mysterious
                                                        thought,
Watched her those seamless faces from the valley's mural girth
As she murmured, 'Oh, wandering Oisin, the strength of the
                                                bell-branch is naught,
For moveth alive in thy fingers the fluttering sadness of earth.

'Then go through the lands in the saddle, and see what the mortal
                                                        men do,
And softly come to thy Niam over the tops of the tide;
But weep for thy. Niam, oh Oisin, weep; for if only thy shoe
Brush lightly as hay-mouse earth's pebbles, no more shalt thou be
                                                        by my side.

'Oh, flaming lion of the world, oh, when wilt thou turn to thy rest?'
I saw from a distant saddle; from the earth she made her moan –
'I would die like a small withered leaf in the autumn, for breast
                                                        unto breast
We shall mingle no more, nor our gazes empty their sweetness lone

'In the isles of the farthest seas where only the spirits come.
Were the winds less soft than the breath of a pigeon who sleeps on
                                                        her nest,
Nor lost in the star-fires and odours the sound of the sea's vague drum?
Oh, flaming lion of the world, oh, when wilt thou turn to thy rest?'

The wailing grew distant; I rode by the woods of the wrinkling bark,
Where ever is murmurous dropping – old silence and that one sound;
For no live creatures live there, no weasels move in the dark –
In reverie forgetful of all things, over the bubbling ground.

And I rode by the plains of the sea's edge, where all is barren and grey,
Grey sands on the green of the grasses and over the dripping trees,
Dripping and doubling landward, as though they would hasten away
Like an army of old men longing for rest from the moan of the seas.

And the winds made the sands on the sea's edge turning and
                                                turning go,
As my mind made the names of the Fenians. Far from the hazel
                                                and oak
I rode away on the surges, where high as the saddle bow
Fled foam underneath me, and round me a wandering and milky smoke.

Long fled the foam-flakes around me, the winds fled out of the vast,
Snatching the bird in secret, nor knew I, embosomed apart,
When they froze the cloth on my body like armour riveted fast,
For Remembrance, lifting her leanness, keened in the gates of my heart.

Till fattening the winds of the morning, an odour of new-mown hay
Came, and my forehead fell low, and my tears like berries fell down;
Later a sound came, half lost in the sound of a shore far away,
From the great grass-barnacle calling, and later the shore-weeds brown.

If I were as I once was, the gold hooves crushing the sands and the
                                                shells
Coming forth from the sea like the morning with red lips
                                                murmuring a song,
Not coughing, my head on my knees, and praying, and wroth with
                                                the bells,
I would leave no saint's head on his body, though spacious his
                                                lands were and strong.

Making way from the kindling surges, I rode on a bridle-path,
Much wondering to see upon all hands, of wattles and wood-work
                                                made,
Thy bell-mounted churches, and guardless the sacred cairn and the
                                                rath,
And a small and a feeble populace stooping with mattock and spade,

Or weeding or ploughing with faces a-shining with much-toil wet;
And in this place and that place, with bodies unglorious, their
                                                chieftains stood,
Awaiting in patience the straw-death, crosiered one, caught in thy net –
Went the laughter of scorn from my mouth like the roaring of
                                                wind in a wood.

And because I went by them so huge and so speedy, with eyes so bright,
Came after the hard gaze of youth, or was lifted an old man's mild head.
And I rode and I rode, and I cried out, 'The Fenians hunt wolves
                    in the night,
So sleep they by daytime.' A voice cried, 'The Fenians a long time
                    are dead.'

A whitebeard stood hushed on the pathway, the flesh of his face as
                    dried grass
And in folds round his eyes and his mouth, he sad as a child
                    without milk;
And the dreams of the islands went out of me, and I knew how
                    men pass,
And their hounds, and their steeds, and their loves, and their
                    youth, and their eyes soft as silk.

And wrapping my face in my hair, I murmured, 'In old age they ceased,'
And my tears were large like to berries, and I murmured, 'Where
                    white clouds lie spread
On Crevroe or on broad Knockfefin, with many of old they fast
On the floors of the gods.' He cried, 'Nay, the gods a long time
                    are dead.'

And shivering and lonely, and longing for Niam, I turned me about,
The heart in me longing to leap like a grasshopper into her heart,
And rode on till over the world's rim floated the sea's old shout,
And mixed with the sound of that roarer the sound of two
                    stumbling apart.

With sweating, with staggering, they lifted and shouldered a sack
                    full of sand,
But prone on the pathway, prone struggling, they lay 'neath the
                    sand-sack at length.
Leaning forth from the gem-studded saddle, I flung it five yards
                    with my hand
With a sob – for men waxing so weakly, a sob for the Fenians' old
                    strength.

The rest thou hast heard of, thou crosiered one – how, when
                                        divided the girth,
I fell on the path, and the horse went away like a summer fly;
And my years three hundred fell on me, and I rose and walked on
                                        the earth,
A creeping old man, full of sleep, with the spittle on his beard
                                        never dry.

How the men of the sand-sack led me to Shaul, with its belfry in air –
Sorry place, where for swing of the war-axe in my dim eyes the
                                        crosier gleams;
What place have Caolte and Fin, and Bran, Sgeolan, Lomair?
Speak, thou too art old with thy memories, an old man surrounded
                                        with dreams.

PATRICK

Where the flesh of the footsole clingeth on the burning stones is
                                        their place;
Where the demons whip them with wires on the burning stones of
                                        wide hell,
Watching the blessed ones move far off, and the smile on God's face,
Between them a gateway of brass and the howl of the angels who fell.

OISIN

Put the staff in my hands; I will go to the Fenians, thou cleric, and
                                        chant
The war-songs that roused them of old; they will rise, making
                                        clouds with their breath
Innumerable, singing, exultant – the clay underneath them shall pant,
And demons, all broken in pieces, be trampled beneath them in death.

And demons afraid in their darkness – deep horror of eyes and of wings,
Afraid their ears on the earth laid, shall listen and rise up and weep
Hearing the shaking of shields and the quiver of stretched bowstrings,
Hearing hell loud with a murmur, as shouting and mocking we sweep.

We will tear out the red flaming stones, and will batter the gateway
                                                            of brass
And enter, and none sayeth 'nay' when there enters the strongly
                                                    armed guest;
Make clean as a broom cleans, and march on as oxen move over
                                                    young grass;
Then feast, making converse of Eri, of wars, and of old wounds
                                                    and rest.

PATRICK

On the red flaming stones without refuge the limbs of the Fenians
                                                        are tost;
No live man goes thither, and no man may war with the strong
                                                    spirits wage;
But weep thou, and wear thou the flags with thy knees, for thy
                                                    soul that is lost,
For thy youth without peace, and thy years with the demons, and
                                            the godless fires of thine age.

OISIN

Ah me! to be old without succour, a show unto children, a stain,
Without laughter, a coughing, alone with remembrance and fear,
All emptied of purple hours as a beggar's cloak in the rain,
As a grass seed crushed by a pebble, as a wolf sucked under a weir.

I will pray no more with the smooth stones: when life in my body
                                                    has ceased —
For lonely to move 'mong the soft eyes of best ones a sad thing were —
I will go to the house of the Fenians, be they in flames or at feast,
To Fin, Caolte, and Conan, and Bran, Sgeolan, Lomair.

Time and the Witch Vivien

A marble-flagged, pillared room. Magical instruments in one corner. A
fountain in the centre.

Vivien (looking down into the fountain). Where moves there any
beautiful as I,
Save, with the little golden greedy carp,
Gold unto gold, a gleam in its long hair,
My image yonder? (*Spreading her hand over the water.*) Ah, my
beautiful,
What roseate fingers! (*Turning away.*) No; nor is there one
Of equal power in spells and secret rites.
The proudest or most coy of spirit things,
Hide where he will, in wave or wrinkled moon,
Obeys.
Some fierce magician flies or walks
Beyond the gateway – by the sentries now –
Close and more close – I feel him in my heart –
Some great one. No; I hear the wavering steps
Without there of a little, light old man;
I dreamt some great one. (*Catching sight of her image, and spreading*
her hand over the water.) Ah, my beautiful,
What roseate fingers!

Enter TIME *as an old pedlar, with a scythe, an hour-glass, and a black bag.*

Ha, ha! ha, ha, ha!
The wrinkled squanderer of human wealth.
Come here. Be seated now; I'd buy of you.
Come, father.
Time. Lady, I nor rest nor sit.
Vivien. Well then, to business; what is in your bag?
Time (putting the bag and hour-glass on the table and resting on his
scythe). Grey hairs and crutches, crutches and grey hairs,
Mansions of memories and mellow thoughts
Where dwell the minds of old men having peace,

And –

Vivien. No; I'll none of these, old Father Wrinkles.

Time. Some day you'll buy them, maybe.

Vivien. Never!

Time (laughing). Never?

Vivien. Why do you laugh?

Time. I laugh the last always.

[*She lays the hour-glass on one side.* TIME *rights it again.*

Vivien. I do not need your scythe. May that bring peace
To those your 'mellow' wares have wearied out.
I'd buy your glass.

Time. My glass I will not sell.
Without my glass I'd be a sorry clown.

Vivien. Yet whiter beard have you than Merlin had.

Time. No taste have I for slumber 'neath an oak.

Vivien. When were you born?

Time. Before your grandam Eve.

Vivien. Oh, I am weary of that foolish tale.
They say you are a gambler and a player
At chances and at moments with mankind.
I'll play you for your old hour-glass. (*Pointing to the instruments of magic.*) You see
I keep such things about me; they are food
For antiquarian meditation. [*Brings dice.*

Time. Ay,
We throw three times.

Vivien. Three-six.

Time. Four-six.

Vivien. Five-six. Ha, Time!

Time. Double sixes!

Vivien. I lose! They're loaded dice. Time always plays
With loaded dice. Another chance! Come, father;
Come to the chess, for young girls' wits are better
Than old men's any day, as Merlin found.

[*Places the chess-board on her knees.*

The passing of those little grains is snow
Upon my soul, old Time.

[*She lays the hour-glass on its side.*

Time. No; thus it stands. [*Rights it again.*

For other stakes we play. You lost the glass.
Vivien. Then give me triumph in my many plots.
Time. Defeat is death.
*Vivie*n. Should my plots fail I'd die.   [*They play.*
Thus play we first with pawns, poor things and weak;
And then the great ones come, and last the king.
So men in life and I in magic play;
First dreams, and goblins, and the lesser sprites,
And now with Father Time I'm face to face.   [*They play.*
I trap you.
Time.   Check.
Vivien.   I do miscalculate.
I am dull to-day, or you were now all lost.
Chance, and not skill, has favoured you, old father!   [*She plays.*
Time. Check.
Vivien.   Ah! how bright your eyes. How swift your moves.
How still it is! hear the carp go splash,
And now and then a bubble rise. I hear
A bird walk on the doorstep.   [*She plays.*
Time.   Check once more.
Vivien. I must be careful now. I have such plots –
Such war plots, peace plots, love plots – every side;
I cannot go into the bloodless land
Among the whimpering ghosts.
Time.   Mate thus.
Vivien.   Already?
Chance hath a skill!   [*She dies.*

The Stolen Child

Where dips the rocky highland
  Of Slewth Wood in the lake,
There lies a leafy island
  Where flapping herons wake
The drowsy water rats;
There we've hid our fairy vats
Full of berries
And of reddest stolen cherries.
Come away, O human child!
To the woods and waters wild
With a fairy, hand in hand,
For the world's more full of weeping than you can understand.

Where the wave of moonlight glosses
  The dim grey sands with light,
Far off by furthest Rosses
  We foot it all the night,
Weaving olden dances,
Mingling hands and mingling glances
  Till the moon has taken flight;
To and fro we leap
  And chase the frothy bubbles,
  While the world is full of troubles
And is anxious in its sleep.
Come away, O human child!
To the woods and waters wild
With a fairy, hand in hand,
For the world's more full of weeping than you can understand.

Where the wandering water gushes
  From the hills above Glen-Car,
In pools among the rushes
  That scarce could bathe a star,
We seek for slumbering trout,
  And whispering in their ears

We give them evil dreams,
  Leaning softly out
    From ferns that drop their tears
    Of dew on the young streams.
Come, O human child!
  To the woods and waters wild
  With a fairy, hand in hand,
For the world's more full of weeping than you can understand.

Away with us he's going,
  The solemn-eyed –
He'll hear no more the lowing
  Of the calves on the warm hillside,
Or the kettle on the hob
  Sing peace into his breast,
Or see the brown mice bob
  Round and round the oatmeal chest.
For he comes, the human child,
  To the woods and waters wild
  With a fairy, hand in hand,
For the world's more full of weeping than he can understand.

Girl's Song

Full moody is my love and sad,
  His moods bow low his sombre crest;
I hold him dearer than the glad,
  And he shall slumber on my breast.

My love hath many a ruthless mood,
  Ill words for all things soft and fair;
I hold him dearer than the good –
  My fingers feel his amber hair.

No tender wisdom floods the eyes
    That watch me with their suppliant light;
I hold him dearer than the wise,
    And for him make me wise and bright.

Ephemera

An Autumn Idyl

'Your eyes that once were never weary of mine
Lie now half hidden under pendulous lids,
Veiled in a dreamy sorrow for their love
That wanes.' 'Ah, wistful voice,' replied the other,
'Though our sad love is fading, let us yet
Stand by the border of the lake once more,
Together in that hour of gentleness
When the poor tired child, passion, falls asleep.
How far away the stars seem, and how far
Is our first kiss, and ah, how old my heart!'
Pensive they paced along the faded leaves,
While slowly answered he whose hand held hers –
'Often has passion worn our wandering hearts,
Earth's aliens. Why so sorrowful? Our souls
Shall warm their lives at many a rustling flame.'

The woods were round them, and the yellow leaves
Fell like faint meteors in the gloom, and once
A rabbit old and lame limped down the path –
Autumn was over him – and now they stood
On the lone border of the sullen lake.
Turning, he saw that she had thrust dead leaves,
Gathered in silence, dewy as her eyes,
In bosom and hair.
              Then he: 'Let us not mourn
That we are tired, for other loves await us.
Hate on and love through unrepining hours.

Before us lies eternity; our souls
Are love, and a continual farewell.'

He spake once more and fondled with his lips
That word of the soul's peace – 'Eternity.'

The little waves that walked in evening whiteness,
Glimmering in her drooped eyes, saw her lips move
And whisper, 'The innumerable reeds
I know the word they cry, "Eternity!"
And sing from shore to shore, and every year
They pine away and yellow and wear out,
And ah, they know not, as they pine and cease,
Not they are the eternal – 'tis the cry.'

An Indian Song

Oh wanderer in the southern weather,
    Our isle awaits us; on each lea
The pea-hens dance, in crimson feather
    A parrot swaying on a tree
    Rages at his own image in the enamelled sea.

There dreamy Time lets fall his sickle
    And Life the sandals of her fleetness,
And sleek young Joy is no more fickle,
    And Love is kindly and deceitless,
    And all is over save the murmur and the sweetness.

There we will moor our lonely ship
    And wander ever with woven hands,
Murmuring softly, lip to lip,
    Along the grass, along the sands –
    Murmuring how far away are all earth's feverish lands:

How we alone of mortals are
   Hid in the earth's most hidden part,
While grows our love an Indian star,
   A meteor of the burning heart,
   One with the waves that softly round us laugh and dart;

One with the leaves; one with the dove
   That moans and sighs a hundred days;
 – How when we die our shades will rove,
   Dropping at eve in coral bays
   A vapoury footfall on the ocean's sleepy blaze,

Kanva, the Indian, on God

I passed along the water's edge below the humid trees,
My spirit rocked in evening's hush, the rushes round my knees,
My spirit rocked in sleep and sighs; and saw the moorfowl pace
All dripping on a grassy slope, and saw them cease to chase
Each other round in circles; and I heard the eldest speak: –
'Who holds the world between His bill and makes us strong or weak
Is an undying moorfowl, and He lives beyond the sky,
The rains are from His dripping wing, the moonbeams from His eye.'
I passed a little further on and heard a lotus talk: –
'Who made the world and ruleth it, He hangeth on a stalk,
For I am in His image made, and all this tinkling tide
Is but a sliding drop of rain between His petals wide.'
A little way within the gloom a roebuck raised his eyes
Brimful of starlight, and he said, 'The Stamper of the Skies,
He is a gentle roebuck; for how else, I pray, could He
Conceive a thing so sad and soft, a gentle thing like me?'
I passed a little further and I heard a peacock say: –
'Who made the grass and made the worms and made my feathers gay,
He is a monstrous peacock, and He waveth all the night
His languid tail above us, lit with myriad spots of light.'

Kanva on Himself

Now wherefore hast thou tears innumerous?
  Hast thou not known all sorrow and delight
Wandering of yore in forests rumorous,
  Beneath the flaming eyeballs of the night,

And as a slave been wakeful in the halls
  Of Rajas and Mahrajas beyond number?
Hast thou not ruled among the gilded walls?
  Hast thou not known a Raja's dreamless slumber?

Hast thou not sat of yore upon the knees
  Of myriads of beloveds, and on thine
Have not a myriad swayed below strange trees
  In other lives? Hast thou not quaffed old wine

By tables that were fallen into dust
  Ere yonder palm commenced his thousand years?
Is not thy body but the garnered rust
  Of ancient passions and of ancient fears?

Then wherefore fear the usury of Time,
  Or Death that cometh with the next life-key?
Nay, rise and flatter her with golden rhyme,
  For as things were so shall things ever be.

Jealousy

SCENE: *A little Indian temple in the Golden Age. Around it a garden; around that again the forest.*
ANASHUYA, *the young priestess, kneeling within.*

Anashuya. Send peace on all the lands and flickering corn. –
Oh, may tranquillity beside him go,
As in the woods he wanders, if he love
No other. – Hear, and may the indolent flocks
Be plenty. – If he gives another love,
May panthers end him. – Hear, and load our king
With wisdom hour by hour. – May we two stand,
When we are dead, beyond the setting suns,
A little from the other shades apart,
With mingling hair, and play upon one lute.
Vijaya (her lover, entering and throwing a lily at her). Hail! hail, my
Anashuya.
Anashuya. Nay; be still.
I, priestess of this temple, offer up
Prayers for the land.
Vijaya. Pray on, and I will wait you, Amrita.
Anashuya. Draw you near, and 'neath yon pillar
Stand you. By Brahma's ever-rustling robe,
Who is Amrita? Woe! ah, woe is me!
Some other fills your mind.
Vijaya. My mother's name.
Anashuya (sings coming out of the temple).

  A sad, sad thought went by me slowly –
Sigh, oh ye little stars! oh, sigh and shake your blue apparel!
  The sad, sad thought has gone from me now wholly –
Sing, oh ye little stars! oh, sing, and raise your rapturous carol
To mighty Brahma – he who made ye many as the sands,
And laid ye on the gates of evening with his quiet hands.
[Sits down on the steps of the temple.

Vijaya, I have brought my evening rice;

The sun hath laid his chin on the grey wood,
Weary, with all his poppies gathered round him.
Vijaya. The hour when Kama,* with a sumptuous smile,
Rises and showers abroad his fragrant arrows,
Piercing the twilight with their murmuring barbs.
Anashuya. See how the sacred old flamingoes come,
Painting with shadow all the marble steps;
Aged and wise, they seek their wonted perches
Within the temple, devious walking, made
To wander by their melancholy minds.
Yon tall one eyes my supper; swiftly chase him
Far, far away. I've named him after you.
He is a famous fisher; hour by hour
He ruffles with his bill the minnowed streams.
Ah! there he snaps my rice. I told you so.
Now cuff him off. He's off! A kiss for you,
Because you saved my rice. Have you no thanks?
Vijaya (sings).

   Sing ye of her, oh first few stars,
Whom Brahma, touching with his finger, praises, for ye hold
The van of wandering quiet; ere ye be too calm and old,
   Sing, turning in your cars,
Sing, till ye raise your hands and sigh, and o'er your car heads peer
With all your whirling hair, and drop through space an azure tear.

Anashuya. What know the pilots of the stars of tears?
Vijaya. Their faces are all worn, and in their eyes
Flashes the fire of sadness, for they see
The icicles that famish all the north,
Where men lie frozen in the glimmering snow;
They see in flaming forests cower the lion
And lioness, with all their whimpering cubs,
And, ever pacing on the verge of things,
The phantom, Beauty, in a mist of tears;
While we alone have round us woven woods,

* The Indian Cupid.

And feel the softness of each other's hands,
Amrita, while –
Anashuya (*going away from him*). Ah me, you love another,

[*Bursting into tears.*

And may some dreadful ill befall her quick!
Vijaya. I loved another; now I love no other.
Among the mouldering of ancient woods
You live, and on the border of the village she,
The daughter of the grey old wood–cutter,
Amrita. This same eve she watched me pass.
Anashuya. Vijaya, swear to love her never more.
Vijaya. Ay, ay.
Anashuya.   Swear by the parents of the gods,
Dread oath, who dwell on sacred Himalay –
On the far Golden Peak – enormous shapes,
Who still were old when the great sea was young;
On their vast faces mystery and dreams;
Their hair along the mountains rolled and filled
From year to year by the unnumbered nests
Of aweless birds, and round their stirless feet
The joyous flocks of deer and antelopes,
Who never heard the unforgiving hound.
Swear!
Vijaya, By the parents of the gods, I swear.
Anashuya (*sings*).

   I have forgiven. O new star!
Maybe you have not heard of us, you have come forth so newly;
   You hunter of the fields afar!
Ah, you will know my loved one by his hunter's arrows truly.
Shoot on him shafts of quietness, that he may ever keep
An inner laughter, and may kiss his hands to me in sleep.

Farewell, Vijaya. Nay, no word, no word;
I, priestess of this temple, offer up
Prayers for the land.

[VIJAYA *goes.*

      Oh, Brahma, guard in sleep
The merry lambs and all the kine complacent,

The flies below the leaves, and the young mice
In the tree roots, and all thy sacred flocks
Of red flamingo; and my love, Vijaya,
May never restless fay with fidget finger
Trouble his sleeping – give him dreams of me.

Song of the Last Arcadian

(He carries a sea-shell)

The woods of Arcady are dead,
And over is their antique joy;
Of old the world on dreaming fed;
Grey Truth is now her painted toy;
Yet still she turns her restless head.
But oh, sick children of the world,
Of all the many changing things
In dreary dancing past us whirled,
To the old cracked tune that Chronos sings,
Words alone are certain good.
Where are now the warring kings,
Word be-mockers? – By the rood,
Where are now the old kings hoary?
They were of no wordy mood;
An idle word is now their glory,
By the stammering schoolboy said,
In the verse of Attic story
Chronicling chimaeras fled.
The very world itself may be
Only a sudden flaming word,
'Mid clanging space a moment heard
In the universe's reverie.
Then nowise worship dusty deeds,
Nor seek – for this is also sooth –
To hunger fiercely after truth,
Lest all thy toiling only breeds

New dreams, new dreams; there is no truth
Saving in thine own heart. Seek, then,
No learning from the starry men,
Who follow with the optic glass
The whirling ways of stars that pass —
Seek then, for this is also sooth,
No word of theirs — the cold star-bane
Has torn and rent their hearts in twain,
And dead is all their human truth.
Go gather by the humming sea
Some twisted, echo-harbouring shell,
And to its lips thy story tell,
And they thy comforters will be,
Rewording in melodious guile
Thy fretful words a little while,
Till they shall singing fade in ruth;
For ruth and joy have brotherhood,
And words alone are certain good —
Sing then, for this is also sooth.
I must be gone — there is a grave
Where daffodil and lily wave,
And downy bees have ambuscade,
And birdly iteration is
Through all the well-beloved glade.
Farewell; I must be gone, I-wis,
That I may soothe that hapless faun
(Who's buried in the sleepy ground),
With mirthful songs till rise the dawn.
His shouting days with mirth were crowned,
And still I dream he treads the lawn,
Walking ghostly 'mong the dew,
Pierced by my glad singing through,
My songs of old earth's dreamy youth.
But ah! she dreams not now — dream thou!
For fair are poppies on the brow:
Dream, dream, for this is also sooth.

King Goll

Mine was a chair of skins and gold,
  Wolf-breeding mountains, galleried Eman,
Mine were clan Morna's tribes untold,
  Many a landsman, many a seaman.
Chaired in a cushioned otter-skin,
  Fields fattening slow, men wise in joy,
I ruled and ruled my life within,
  Peace-making, mild, a kingly boy.
And every whispering old man said,
Bending low his fading head,
'This young man brings the age of gold.'
(They will not hush, the leaves a-flutter round me – the
                                        beech-leaves old).

Splashed all with clay and journey dull,
  Cried a herald, 'To our valleys
Comes a sea-king masterful
  To fill with cows his hollow galleys.'
From rolling valley and rivery glen,
  With horsemen hurrying near and far,
I drew at evening my mailed men,
  And under the blink o' the morning star
Fell on the pirates by the deep,
And they inherit the great sleep.
These hands slew many a seaman bold.
(They will not hush, the leaves a-flutter round me – the
                                        beech-leaves old.)

But slowly as I shouting slew
  And trampled in the bubbling mire,
In my most secret spirit grew
  A fever and a whirling fire.
I paused – the stars above me shone,
  And shone around the eyes of men;

I paused – and far away rushed on,
  Over the heath and spongy fen,
And crumpled in my hands the staff
Of my long spear with scream and laugh
And song that down the valleys rolled.
(They will not hush, the leaves a-flutter round me – the
                                        beech-leaves old).

And now I wander in the woods
  Where summer gluts the golden bees,
Or in autumnal solitudes
  Arise the leopard-coloured trees;
Or where along the wintry strands
  The cormorants shiver on their rocks,
I wander on and wave my hands,
  And sing and shake my heavy locks.
The grey wolf knows me; by one ear
I lead along the woodland deer,
And hares run near me growing bold.
(They will not hush, the leaves a-flutter round me – the
                                        beech-leaves old.)

Once, while within a little town
  That slumbered 'neath the harvest moon,
I passed a-tiptoe up and down,
  Murmuring a mountain tune
Of how I hear on hill heads high
  A tramping of tremendous feet.
I saw this harp all songless lie
  Deserted in a doorway seat,
And bore it to the woods with me.
Of some unhuman misery
Our married voices wildly trolled.
(They will not hush, the leaves a-flutter round me – the
                                        beech-leaves old.)

And toads, and every outlawed thing,
　　With eyes of sadness rose to hear,
From pools and rotting leaves, me sing
　　The song of outlaws and their fear.
My singing sang me fever-free;
　　My singing fades, the strings are torn;
I must away by wood and sea
　　And lift an ulalu forlorn,
And fling my laughter to the sun
　　– For my remembering hour is done –
In all his evening vapours rolled.
(They will not hush, the leaves a-flutter round me –　the
　　　　　　　　　　　　　　　　　　　beech-leaves old.)

The Meditation of the Old Fisherman

Ye waves, though ye dance 'fore my feet like children at play,
　　Though ye glow and ye glance, though ye purr and ye dart,
In the Junes that were warmer than these are, the waves were more
　　　　　　　　　　　　　　　　　　　　　　　　gay
　　When I was a boy with never a crack in my heart.

The lines are not heavy, nor heavy the long nets brown –
　　Ah me! full many a creak gave the creel in the cart
That carried the fish for the sale in the far-away town,
　　When I was a boy with never a crack in my heart.

And ah, ye proud maidens, ye are not so fair, when *his* oar
　　Is heard on the water, as they were, the proud and apart,
Who paced in the eve by the nets on the pebbly shore,
　　When I was a boy with never a crack in my heart.

The Ballad of Moll Magee

Come round me, little childer;
  There, don't fling stones at me
Because I mutter as I go,
  But pity Moll Magee.

My husband was a fisher poor
  With shore lines in the say;
My work was saltin' herrings
  The whole of the long day.

Times from the saltin' shed,
  Along the pebbly street,
Home in the blessed moonlight
  I scarce could drag my feet.

I'd always been but weakly,
  And my baby was just born;
A neighbour minded her by day,
  I minded her till morn.

I lay upon my baby,
  Ye little childer dear,
I looked on my cold baby
  In the frosty mornin' clear.

A weary woman sleeps so hard!
  My husband stood up pale,
And gave me money, and bade me go
  To my own place, Kinsale.

He drove me forth and shut the door,
  And gave his curse to me;
I went away in silence,
  No neighbour could I see.

The windows and the doors were shut,
  One star shone faint and green;
The little straws were turnin' round
  Across the bare boreen.

I went away in silence:
  Beyond old Martin's wood,
A-blowin' of her mornin' fire,
  I saw a neighbour good.

She drew from me my story –
  My money's all used up,
And still, with pityin', scornin' eye,
  She gives me bite and sup.

She says my husband sure will come
  And fetch me home agin;
But always, as I'm movin' round,
  Without doors or within,

A-pilin' wood or pilin' turf,
  Or goin' to the well,
I'm thinking of my baby
  And keenin' to mysel'.

And sometimes I am sure she knows,
  When, opening wide His door,
God lights the stars, His candles,
  And looks upon the poor.

So now, ye little childer,
  Ye won't fling stones at me,
But gather with your shinin' looks
  And pity Moll Magee.

The Phantom Ship

Flames the shuttle of the lightning across the driving sleet,
Ay, and shakes in sea-green waverings along the fishers' street;
Gone the stars and gone the white moon, gone and puffed away
                                                and dead.
Never storm arose so swiftly; scarce the children were in bed,
Scarce the old and wizen houses had their doors and windows shut.
Ah! it dwelt within the twilight as the worm within the nut,
'Waken, waken, sleepy fishers; no hour is this for sleep,'
Cries a voice at roaring midnight beside the moonless deep.
Half dizzy with the lightning there runs a gathering band –
'Watcher, wherefore have ye called us?' Eyes go after his lean hand,
And the fisher men and women from the dripping harbour wall
See the darkness slow disgorging a vessel blind with squall.
'Bring the ropes now! Stand ye by now! See, she rounds the
                                                harbour clear.
God! they're mad to fly such canvas!' Ah! what bell-notes do they hear?
Say what ringer rings at midnight; for, in the belfry high,
Slow the chapel bell is tolling as though the dead passed by.
Round she comes in stays before them; cease the winds, and on
                                                their poles
Cease the sails their flapping uproar, and the hull no longer rolls.
Now a scream from all those fishers, for there on deck there be
All the drowned that ever were drowned from that village by the sea;
And the ghastly ghost-flames glimmer all along the taffrail rails
On the drowned men's hands and faces, on the spars and on the sails.
Hush'd the fishers, till a mother calls by name her drownèd son;
Then each wife and maid and mother calls by name some drownèd
                                                one.
Stands each grey and silent phantom on the same regardless spot –
Joys and fears in their grey faces that the live earth knoweth not;
Down the vapours fall and hide them from the children of a day,
And the winds come down and blow them with the vapours far away.
Hang the mist-threads for a little while like cobwebs in the air;
Then the stars grow out of heaven with their countenances fair.

'Pray for the souls in purgatory,' the pale priest trembling cries.

Prayed those forgotten fishers, till in the eastern skies
Came olive fires of morning and on the darkness fed,
By the slow heaving ocean – mumbling mother of the dead.

A Lover's Quarrel among the Fairies

A moonlit moor. Fairies leading a child.

MALE FAIRIES

Do not fear us, earthly maid!
    We will lead you hand in hand
By the willows in the glade,
    By the gorse on the high land,

By the pasture where the lambs
    Shall awake with lonely bleat,
Shivering closer to their dams
    From the rustling of our feet.

You will with the banshee chat,
    And will find her good at heart,
Sitting on a warm smooth mat
    In the green hill's inmost part.

We will bring a crown of gold,
    Bending humbly every knee,
Now thy great white doll to hold –
    Oh, so happy would we be!

Ah! it is so very big,
    And we are so very small!
So, we dance a fairy jig
    To the fiddle's rise and fall.

Yonder see the fairy girls
  All their jealousy display,
Lift their chins and toss their curls,
  Lift their chins and turn away.

See you, brother, Cranberry Fruit —
  Ho! ho! ho! the merry blade! —
Hugs and pets and pats yon newt,
  Teasing every wilful maid.

GIRL FAIRIES

Lead they one with foolish care,
  Deafening us with idle sound —
One whose breathing shakes the air,
  One whose footfall shakes the ground.

Come you, Coltsfoot, Mousetail, come!
  Come I know where, far away,
Owls there be whom age makes numb;
  Come and tease them till the day.

Puffed like puff-balls on a tree,
  Scoff they at the modern earth —
Ah! how large mice used to be
  In their days of youthful mirth!

Come, beside a sandy lake,
  Feed a fire with stems of grass;
Roasting berries steam and shake —
  Talking hours swiftly pass!

Long before the morning fire
  Wake the larks upon the green.
Yonder foolish ones will tire
  Of their tall, new-fangled queen.

They will lead her home again
  To the orchard-circled farm;

At the house of weary men.
  Raise the door-pin with alarm,

And come kneeling on one knee,
  While we shake our heads and scold
This their wanton treachery,
  And our slaves be as of old.

Mosada

'And my Lord Cardinal hath had strange days in his youth.'
Extract from a Memoir of the Fifteenth Century

MOSADA, *a Moorish lady*
EBREMAR, *a monk*
COLA, *a lame boy*
MONKS *and* INQUISITORS

SCENE I

A little Moorish room in the village of Azubia. In the centre of the room
a chafing-dish.

MOSADA *alone.*

Mosada. Three times the roses have grown less and less,
And thrice the peaches flushed upon the walls,
And thrice the corn around the sickles flamed,
Since 'mong my people, tented on the hills,
Where they all summer feed their wandering flocks,
He stood a messenger. In April's prime
(Swallows were flashing their white breasts above
Or perching on the tents, a-weary still
From waste seas cross'd, yet ever garrulous)
Along the velvet vale I saw him come –

Feet of dark Gomez, where now wander ye?
In autumn, when far down the mountain slopes
The heavy clusters of the grapes were full,
I saw him sigh and turn and pass away;
For I and all my people were accurst
Of his sad God; and down among the grass
Hiding my face, I cried long, bitterly.
'Twas evening, and the cricket nation sang
Around my head and danced among the grass;
And all was dimness, till a dying leaf
Slid circling down and softly touched my lips
With dew, as though 'twere sealing them for death.
Yet somewhere in the footsore world we meet,
We two, before we die; for Azolar,
The star-taught Moor, said thus it was decreed
By those wan stars that sit in company
Above the Alpujarras on their thrones:
That when the stars of our nativity
Draw star to star, as on that eve he passed
Down the long valleys from my people's tents,
We meet – we two. (*She opens the casement. A sound of laughter floats
in.*) How merry all these are
Among the fruit! But there, lame Cola crouches
Away from all the others. Now the sun
Sinks, shining on the little crucifix
Hung on his doublet – dear and mournful child,
Seër of visions! Now eve falls asleep,
The hour of incantation comes a-tiptoe,
And Cola, seeing, knows the sign and comes.
Thus do I burn these precious herbs, whose smoke
Pours up and floats in fragrance round my head
In coil on coil of azure.

Enter COLA.

All is ready.

Cola. I will not share your sin.
Mosada.   This is no sin.
No sin to see in coil on coil of azure

Pictured, where wander the beloved feet
Whose footfall I have longed for, three sad summers.
Why these new fears?
Cola.   The great monk Ebremar,
The dark still man, has come and says 'tis sin.
Mosada. They say the wish itself is half the sin;
Then has this one been sinned full many times.
Yet 'tis no sin; my father taught it me.
He was a man most learned and most mild,
Who, dreaming to a wondrous age, lived on,
Tending the roses round his lattice door.
For years his days had dawned and faded thus
Among the plants; the flowery silence fell
Deep in his soul, like rain upon a soil
Worn by the solstice fierce, and made it pure.
Would he teach any sin?
Cola.   Gaze in the cloud
Yourself.
Mosada. None but the innocent can see.
Cola. They say I am all ugliness; lame-footed
I am; one shoulder turned awry – why then
Should I be good? But you are beautiful.
Mosada. I cannot see.
Cola.   The beetles, and the bats,
And spiders are my friends; I'm theirs, and they are
Not good; but you are like the butterflies.
Mosada. I cannot see! I cannot see! but you
Shall see a thing to talk on when you're old,
Under a lemon tree beside your door;
And all the elders sitting in the sun
Will wondering listen, and this tale shall ease
For long the burthen of their talking griefs.
Cola. Upon my knees I pray you, let it sleep,
The vision.
Mosada.   You are pale and weeping. Child,
Be not afraid, you'll see no fearful thing.
Thus, thus I beckon from her viewless fields –
Thus beckon to our aid a Phantom fair
And calm, robed all in raiment moony white.

She was a great enchantress once of yore,
Whose dwelling was a tree-wrapt island, lulled
Far out upon the water world and ringed
With wonderful white sands, where never yet
Were furled the wings of ships. There in a dell,
A lily-blanchèd place, she sat and sang,
And in her singing wove around her head
White lilies, and her song flew forth afar
Along the sea; and many a man grew hushed
In his own house or 'mong the merchants grey,
Hearing the far-off singing guile, and groaned,
And manned an argosy and sailing died.
In the far isle she sang herself asleep,
But now I wave her hither to my side.
Cola. Stay, stay, or I will hold your white arms down.
Ah me! I cannot reach them – here and there
Darting you wave them, darting in the vapour.
Heard you? Your lute hung in the window sounded!
I feel a finger drawn across my cheek!
Mosada. The phantoms come; ha! ha! they come, they come!
I wave them hither, my breast heaves with joy.
Ah! now I'm Eastern-hearted once again,
And, while they gather round my beckoning arms,
I'll sing the songs the dusky lovers sing,
Wandering in sultry palaces of Ind,
A lotus in their hands –   [*The door is flung open.*

Enter the OFFICERS OF THE INQUISITION.

First Inquisitor.   Young Moorish girl
Taken in magic, in the Church's name
I here arrest thee.
Mosada.   It was Allah's will.
Touch not this boy, for he is innocent.
Cola. Forgive! for I have told them everything.
They said I'd burn in hell unless I told.
                    [*She turns away – he clings to her dress.*
Forgive me!
Mosada.   It was Allah's will.

Second Inquisitor.   The cords.
Mosada. No need to bind my hands. Where are ye, sirs?
For ye are hid with vapour.
Second Inquisitor.   Round the stake
The vapour is much thicker.
Cola.   God! the stake!
Ye said that ye would fright her from her sin –
No more; take me instead of her, great sirs.
She was my only friend; I'm lame, you know –
One shoulder twisted, and the children cry
Names after me.
First Inquisitor. Lady –
Mosada.   I come.
Cola (following).   Forgive,
Forgive, or I will die.
Mosada (*stooping and kissing him*). 'Twas Allah's will.

SCENE II

*A room in the building of the Inquisition of Granada,
lighted by a stained window, picturing St James of Spain.*

MONKS *and* INQUISITORS.

First Monk. Will you not hear my last new song?
First Inquisitor.   Hush, hush!
So she must burn, you say?
Second Inquisitor.   She must in truth.
First Inquisitor. Will he not spare her life? How would one matter
When there are many?
Second Monk.   Ebremar will stamp
This heathen horde away. You need not hope;
And know you not she kissed that pious child
With poisonous lips, and he is pining since?
First Monk. You're full of wordiness. Come, hear my song.
Second Monk. In truth, an evil race. Why strive for her,
A little Moorish girl?
Second Inquisitor.   Small worth.

First Monk.   My song –
First Inquisitor. I had a sister like her once, my friend.
                    [*Touching the first* MONK *on the shoulder.*
Where is our brother Peter? When you're nigh,
He is not far. I'd have him speak for her.
I saw his jovial mood bring once a smile
To sainted Ebremar's sad eyes. I think
He loves our brother Peter in his heart.
If Peter would but ask her life – who knows?
First Monk. He digs his cabbages. He brings to mind
That song I've made. 'Tis of an Irish tale.
A saint of Munster, when much fasting, saw
This vision of Peter and the burning gate.

(*Sings*)

> I saw a stranger tap and wait
> By the door of Peter's gate,
> Then he shouted, 'Open wide
> Thy sacred door;' but Peter cried,
> 'No, thy home is deepest hell,
> Deeper than the deepest well.'
> Then the stranger softly crew –
> 'Cock-a-doodle-doodle-do!'
> Answered Peter: 'Enter in,
> Friend; but 'twere a deadly sin
> Ever more to speak a word
> Of any unblessed earthly bird.'

First Inquisitor. Be still; I hear the step of Ebremar.
Yonder he comes; bright-eyed, and hollow-cheeked
From fasting – see, the red light slanting down
From the great painted window wraps his brow,
As with an aureole.

           EBREMAR *enters. They all bow to him.*

First Inquisitor. My suit to you –
Ebremar. I will not hear; the Moorish girl must die.
I will burn heresy from this mad earth,

And –
First Inquisitor. Mercy is the manna of the world.
Ebremar. The wages of sin is death.
Second Monk.   No use. No good.
First Inquisitor. My lord, if it must be, I pray descend
Yourself into the dungeon 'neath our feet
And importune with weighty words this Moor,
That she forswear her heresies and save
Her soul from seas of endless flame in hell.
Ebremar. I speak alone with servants of the Cross
And dying men – and yet – But no, farewell.
Second Monk. No use.
Ebremar. Away! (*They go.*) Hear, thou enduring God,
Who giveth to the golden-crested wren
Her hanging mansion. Give to me, I pray,
The burthen of Thy truth. Reach down Thy hands
And fill me with Thy rage, that I may bruise
The heathen. Yea, and shake the sullen kings
Upon their thrones. The lives of men shall flow
As quiet as the little rivulets
Beneath the sheltering shadow of Thy Church;
And Thou shalt bend, enduring God, the knees
Of the great warriors whose names have sung
The world to its fierce infancy again.

SCENE III

*The dungeon of the Inquisition. The morning of the auto-da-fé
dawns dimly through a barred window. A few faint stars are shining.
Swallows are circling in the dimness without.*

MOSADA, *alone.*

Mosada. Oh, swallows, swallows, swallows, will ye fly
This eve, to-morrow, or to-morrow night
Above the farm-house by the little lake
That rustles in the reeds with patient pushes,
Soft as the whispering of a long-lost footstep

Circling the brain? My brothers will pass down
Quite soon the cornfield, where the poppies grow,
To their farm work; how silent all will be!
But no, in this warm weather, 'mong the hills,
Will be the faint far thunder-sound, as though
The world were dreaming in its summer sleep;
That will be later, day is scarcely dawning.
And Hassan will be with them – he was so small,
A weak, thin child, when last I saw him there.
He will be taller now – 'twas long ago.

The men are busy in the glimmering square.
I hear the murmur as they raise the beams
To build the circling seats, where high in air
Soon will the churchmen nod above the crowd.
I'm not of that pale company whose feet
Ere long shall falter through the noisy square,
And not come thence; for here in this small ring –
Hearken, ye swallows! – I have hoarded up
A poison drop. A toy, a fancy once,
A fashion with us Moorish maids, begot
Of dreaming and of watching by the door
The shadows pass; but now, I love my ring,
For it alone of all the world will do
My bidding. (*Sucks poison from the ring.*) Now 'tis done, and I am glad
And free – 'twill thieve away with sleepy mood
My thoughts, and yonder brightening patch of sky
With three bars crossed, and these four walls my world,
And yon few stars grown dim, like eyes of lovers
The noisy world divides. How soon a deed
So small makes one grow weak and tottering!
Where shall I lay me down? That question is
A weighty question, for it is the last.
Not there, for there a spider weaves her web.
Nay here, I'll lay me down where I can watch
The burghers of the night fade one by one.
                              ...Yonder a leaf
Of apple-blossom circles in the gloom,
Floating from yon barred window. Small new-comer,

Thou'rt welcome. Lie there close against my fingers.
I wonder which is whitest, they or thou.
'Tis thou, for they've grown blue around the nails.
My blossom, I am dying, and the stars
Are dying too. They were full seven stars;
Two only now they are, two side by side.

Oh, Allah! it was thus they shone that night
When my lost lover left these arms. My Gomez
We meet at last, the ministering stars
Of our nativity hang side by side,
And throb within the circles of green dawn.
Too late, too late, for I am near to death.
I try to lift mine arms – they fall again.
This death is heavy in my veins like sleep.
I cannot even crawl along the flags
A little nearer those bright stars. Tell me,
Is it your message, stars, that when death comes
My soul shall touch with his, and the two flames
Be one? I think all's finished now and sealed.

After a pause enter EBREMAR.

Ebremar. Young Moorish girl, thy final hour is here;
Cast off thy heresies, and save thy soul
From the undying worm. She sleeps – (*Starting.*) Mosada –
Oh, God! – awake! thou shalt not die. She sleeps,
Her head cast backward in her unloosed hair.
Look up, look up, thy Gomez is by thee.
A fearful paleness creeps across her breast
And out-spread arms. (*Casting himself down by her.*) Be not so pale,
dear love.

Oh, can my kisses bring a flush no more
Upon thy face? How heavily thy head
Hangs on my breast! Listen, we shall be safe.
We'll fly from this before the morning star.
Dear heart, there is a secret way that leads
Its paven length towards the river's marge
Where lies a shallop in the yellow reeds.

Awake, awake, and we will sail afar,
Afar along the fleet white river's face –
Alone with our own whispers and replies –
Alone among the murmurs of the dawn.
Once in thy nation none shall know that I
Was Ebremar, whose thoughts were fixed on God,
And heaven, and holiness.
Mosada.   Let's talk and grieve,
For that's the sweetest music for sad souls.
Day's dead, all flame-bewildered, and the hills
In list'ning silence gazing on our grief.
I never knew an eve so marvellous still.
Ebremar. Her dreams are talking with old years. Awake,
Grieve not, for Gomez kneels beside thee –
Mosada.   Gomez,
'Tis late, wait one more day; below the hills
The foot-worn way is long, and it grows dark.
It is the darkest eve I ever knew.
Ebremar. I kneel by thee – no parting now – look up.
She smiles – is happy with her wandering griefs.
Mosada. So you must go; kiss me before you go.
Oh, would the busy minutes might fold up
Their thieving wings that we might never part.
I never knew a night so honey-sweet.
Ebremar. There is no leave-taking. I go no more.
Safe on the breast of Gomez lies thy head,
Unhappy one.
Mosada.   Go not, go not, go not;
For night comes fast. Look down on me, my love,
And see how thick the dew lies on my face.
I never knew a night so dew-bedrowned.
Ebremar. Oh, hush the wandering music of thy mind.
Look on me once. Why sink your eyelids thus?
Why do you hang so heavy in my arms?
Love, will you die when we have met? One look
Give to thy Gomez.
Mosada.   Gomez – he has gone
From here, along the shadowy way that winds
Companioning the river's pilgrim torch.

I'll see him longer if I stand out here
Upon the mountain's brow. (*She tries to stand and totters.* EBREMAR
　　　supports her, and she stands as if pointing down into a valley.)
　　　　　　　　Yonder he treads
The path o'er-muffled with the leaves – dead leaves,
Like happy thoughts grown sad in evil days.
He fades among the mists; how fast they come,
And pour upon the world! Ah! well-a-day!
Poor love and sorrow, with their arms thrown round
Each other's necks, and whispering as they go,
Still wander through the world. He's gone, he's gone.
I'm weary – weary, and 'tis very cold.
I'll draw my cloak around me; it is cold.
I never knew a night so bitter cold.　　　　　　　　　　　[*Dies.*

　　　　　　　Enter MONKS *and* INQUISITORS.

First Inquisitor. My lord, you called?
Ebremar.　　　　　　　　　　Not I. This maid is dead.
First Monk. From poison; for you cannot trust these Moors.
You're pale, my lord.
First Inquisitor (*aside*). His lips are quivering;
The flame that shone within his eyes but now
Has flickered and gone out.
Ebremar.　　　　　　　　I am not well.
'Twill pass. I'll see the other prisoners now,
And importune their souls to penitence,
So they escape from hell. But, pardon me,
Your hood is threadbare – see that it be changed
Before we take our seats above the crowd.

　　　　　　　　　　　　　　　　　　[*They go out.*

How Ferencz Renyi Kept Silent

Hungary, 1848

We, too, have seen our bravest and our best
To prisons go, and mossy ruin rest
Where homes once whitened vale and mountain crest;
Therefore, O nation of the bleeding breast,
Libations, from the Hungary of the West.

Before his tent the General sips his wine,
Waves off the flies, and warms him in the shine.
The Austrian Haynau he, in many lands
Famous, a man of rules, a victor. Stands
Before him one well guarded, with bound hands;
Schoolmaster he, a dreamer, fiddler, first
In every dance, by children sought. 'Accurst,
Thy name is?'
        'Renyi.'
           'Of?'
              'This village.'
                    'Good!
Hiding the rebels worm in yonder wood
Or yonder mountains. Where? Thou shalt be free –
Silence! Thou shalt be dead!'

               Now suddenly
The spirit of young Renyi has grown old.
He turns where, hung like drops of dripping gold,
Flashing and flickering with ever-undulant wing
About a sun-flushed dove-cot, cooing, cling
The doves whose growing forms he'd watched. Not these
He numbers. He a brown farm-house sees,
Where shadow of cherry, and shadow of apple trees,
Enclose a quiet place of beds box-bordered, bees,
Hives, currant bushes. There his kin are. High
Above, the woods where with the soft mild eye
Of her he loved fixed on him full of light,

Often he had bent down some bough all bright
With berries. Placid as a homeward bee,
Glad, simple – nay, he sought not mystery,
Nor, gazing forth where life's sad sickles reap,
Searched the unsearchable – why good men weep;
Why those who do good often be not good,
Why they who will the highest sometimes brood,
Clogged in a marsh where the slow marsh clay clings,
Abolished by a mire of little things,
Untuned by their own striving.
                                        If one such
Were here, he would turn death into a crutch;
But this one – this one.
                                Now his head drops low,
Drops on his bosom, sombre, moist and slow.
'Choose!' Restless Haynau's fingers tapping go.
This sullen peasant spoils the good sunshine,
This sullen peasant spoils the good red wine.
He whispers to a soldier, who goes out –
A neighbouring cricket lifts his shrilly shout
Reiterant. A bird goes by the tent,
A lizard crawls – the two men gaze intent,
As though they'd vowed to measure all its ways.

Returns that soldier in the evening rays
Half hid. He brings the peasant's only kin,
Two women, withered one and small and thin,
Bent low with toil and hoariest years. The other
Of middle age.
                        'His sister here and mother.'
The soldier thus, and Haynau – 'Peasant, speak
If these be precious.'
                                'I am old and weak,'
That ancient mother cries, 'speak not, my son.
I'm weak, and by the hands shall hold each one
Of my dead children soon, whate'er betide,
For I am old and weak.'

                        And at her side

The sister: 'Sell thy country, and the shame
Of traitor evermore is on our name.'
Haynau, the man of system, lifts his hand
Serene. They're led away, and where a band
Of soldiers ranked is on a grassy spot,
A score of yards off 'neath a willow, shot.

'Now hath he kith or kin, or any friend?'
A soldier answers: 'By the camp's far end
I saw a girl afraid to be too near,
Afraid to be too far.' 'Ay, bring her here!'

Time goes. The flakèd fire of evening crawls
Along the tents, the fields, the village walls.
The hare hath laid asleep her frolic wits,
And every flower above its shadow sits.
'On this embroidered cloud,' the sun hath said,
'A little will I lay my weary head,
Among the gold, the amber, and the red.'
A careful field-mouse finds a fallen crumb;
Now steps draw close, he hides beneath a drum.
That maiden bring they. When the tall red deer
In trouble is, the doe will linger near.
A peasant pale and pretty, her eyes for fear,
Like small brown moths, a-tremble.
                              'Renyi say
Where worm the rebels, or my bullets lay
The young one with the others.' Renyi's pale
But speechless, and the maiden with long wail
Flings her before him. 'Save thyself and me.
Speak, Ferencz, speak. We love each other. See,
I am so young. Dost thou no longer know,
Beloved, how two little years ago
I came the first time to thy village school?
Thou hast forgotten. On the oaken stool
I sat me down beside thee, and I knew
So little. As the months passed by we grew
To love each other. In my prayer-book still
The violets are that on the wooded hill

We gathered. Ferencz, nay, I must not die:
I am to be your wife. A village high
And lost and far in yonder hills I know;
There far away from all we two will go,
And be so happy.'

            To his hands she clings,
With cries and murmurs. Suddenly he flings
Away her clinging hands, and turns. She throws
Her arms around his feet. The signal goes
From Haynau's lifted fingers – two draw nigh
And seize her, and thus floats her quivering cry:
'Assassin, my assassin! thou who let'st me die,
I curse thee – curse thee!'

               Renyi silent stands,
And she is dragged to where the willow bands
With quiet shade its ever dewy-plot.
Noise! and a flash, a momentary blot.
So ends a brain – a world!

              The smoke goes up,
Creeping along the heavens' purple cup,
Higher and higher gold with evening light;
It seems to fondle, with a finger bright
And soft, one glimmering star.

              Renyi has cast
His bonds away, sore struggling.

              Now at last
Haynau, thine hour has come, thy followers far
Beside the willow.

             Nay, to yonder star,
Yon bauble of the heavens, he lifts his hands,
And over tillage fields and pasture lands
Where lies the cow at peace beside her calf,
He rushes, rolling from his lips a madman's laugh.

The Fairy Doctor

The fairy doctor comes our way
  Over the sorrel-covered wold –
Now sadly, now unearthly gay,
  A little withered man, and old.

He knows by signs of secret wit
  The man whose hour of death draws nigh,
And who will moan in the under pit,
  And who foregather in the sky.

He sees the fairy hosting move
  By heath or hollow or rushy mere,
And then his heart fills full of love,
  And full his eyes of fairy cheer.

Cures he hath for cow or goat
  With fairy-smitten udders dry –
Cures for calves with 'plaining throat,
  That sickening near their mothers lie;

And many a herb and many a spell
  For hurts and ails and lover's moan –
For all save him who pining fell,
  Glamoured by fairies for their own.

Now be courteous, now be kind,
  Lest he may some glamour fold
Closely round us, body and mind –
  The little withered man, and old.

Falling of the Leaves

Autumn is over the long leaves that love us,
  And over the mice in the barley sheaves;
Yellow the leaves of the rowan above us,
  And yellow the wet wild-strawberry leaves.

The hour of the waning of love has beset us,
  And weary and worn are our sad souls now;
Let us part, ere the season of passion forget us,
  With a kiss and a tear on thy drooping brow.

Miserrimus

There was a man whom Sorrow named his friend,
  And he, of his high kinsman Sorrow dreaming,
  Went walking with slow steps along the gleaming
And humming sands, where windy surges wend.
He called aloud to all the stars to lend
  Their hearing, and some comfort give, but they
  Among themselves laugh on and sing alway.
Then cried the man whom Sorrow named his friend:
'O sea, old sea, hear thou my piteous story!'
  The sea swept on and cried her old cry still,
  Rolling along in dreams from hill to hill;
And from the persecution of her glory
He fled, and in a far-off valley stopping,
  Cried all his story to the dewdrops glistening.
  But naught they heard, for they are ever listening,
The dewdrops, for the sound of their own dropping.
And then the man whom Sorrow named his friend
  Sought once again the shore, and chose a shell
  And thought, 'To this will I my story tell,

And mine own words re-echoing shall send
Their sadness through the hollows of its heart,
  And mine own tale again for me shall sing,
  And mine own whispering words be comforting,
And lo – my heavy burthen may depart.'
Then sang he softly nigh the pearly rim;
  But the sad dweller by the seaways lone
  Changed all his words to inarticulate moan
Within her wildering whirls – forgetting him.

The Priest and the Fairy

Unto the heart of the woodland straying,
Where the shaking leaf with the beam was playing,

Musingly wandered the village priest.
As the summer voice of the daytime ceased,

He came to the home of the forest people
From where the old ivy crawls round the old steeple,

And under a shady oak-tree sat,
Where the moss was spread like his own doormat.

The tangled thoughts of the finished day
Fled from his brow where the hair was grey;

And as the time to darkness plodded,
He thought wise things as his grey head nodded.

How 'the only good is musing mild,
And evil still is action's child.

'With action all the world is vexed,'
He'd find for this some holy text.

He'd slept among the singing trees,
Among the murmurs of the bees,

A full hour long, when rose a feather
Out of a neighbouring bunch of heather;

And then a pointed face was seen
Beneath a pointed cap of green;

And straight before the sleeping priest
There stood a man, of men the least —

Three spans high as he rose to his feet,
And his hair was as yellow as waving wheat.

Now, what has a fairy to do with a priest
Who is six feet high in his socks at least?

He drew from his cap a feather grey,
On the nose of the sleeper he made it play;

The sleeper awoke with a sudden start,
With open mouth and beating heart.

He had dreamed the cow had got within
His garden ringed with jessamine,

And many a purple gillyflower eaten,
And under her hoofs the marigolds beaten.

Then 'gan to speak that goblin rare,
Brushing back his yellow hair:

'Man of wisdom, from thy sleeping
I have roused thee; for the weeping

'Of our great queen is ever heard
Among the haunts of bee and bird.

'We buried late in a hazel dell
A fairy whom we loved full well;

'The swiftest he to dance or fly
And his hair was as dark as a plover's eye.

Man of wisdom, dost thou know
Where the souls of fairies go?'

The priest looked neither to right nor left,
Nigh of his wits by fear bereft.

'Ave Marie,' muttered he
Over the beads of his rosary.

The fairies' herald spake once more:
'Say and thrice anigh thy door

Every summer wilt thou see
Wild bees' honey laid for thee.'

The father dropt his rosary –
'They are lost, they are lost, each one,' cried he.

And then his heart grew well-nigh dead
Because of the thing his tongue had said.

As a wreath of smoke in wind-blown flight
The fairy vanished from his sight,

And came to where his brethren stood,
Away in the heart of the antique wood;

And when they heard that tale of his
They grew so very still, I wis

Were you a fairy you'd have heard
The breathing of the smallest bird,

The beating of a lev'ret's heart;
And then the fay queen sobbed apart,

And all the sad fay chivalry
Upraised their voices bitterly.

★

A woodman on his homeward way
Heard the voice of their dismay,

And said, 'Yon bittern cries, in truth,
As though his days were full of ruth.

'If I were free to do as little
As dance upon the spear-grass brittle,

'Or seek where sweetest water bubbles,
Remote from all the hard earth troubles,

'And cut no wood the whole day long,
I'd glad folks' hearts with blither song.'

The Fairy Pedant

FIRST FAIRY

Afar from our lawn and our levée,
  O sister of sorrowful gaze!
Where the roses in scarlet are heavy
  And dream of the end of their days,
You move in another dominion
  And hang o'er the historied stone:
Unpruned is your beautiful pinion
  Who wander and whisper alone.

ALL

Come away while the moon's in the woodland,
  We'll dance and then feast in a dairy.
Though youngest of all in our good band,
  You are wasting away, little fairy.

SECOND FAIRY

Ah! cruel ones, leave me alone now
  While I murmur a little and ponder
The history here in the stone now;
  Then away and away will I wander,
And measure the minds of the flowers,
  And gaze on the meadow-mice wary,
And number their days and their hours –

ALL

You are wasting away, little fairy.

SECOND FAIRY

O shining ones, lightly with song pass,
  Ah! leave me, I pray you and beg.
My mother drew forth from the long grass
  A piece of a nightingale's egg,
And cradled me here where are sung,

Of birds even, longings for aery
Wild wisdoms of spirit and tongue.

ALL

You are wasting away, little fairy.

FIRST FAIRY (*turning away*)

Though tenderest roses were round you,
    The soul of the pitiless place
With pitiless magic has bound you –
    Ah! woe for the loss of your face,
And loss of your laugh and its lightness –
    Ah! woe for your wings and your head –
Ah! woe for your eyes and their brightness –
    Ah! woe for your slippers of red.

ALL

Come away while the moon's in the woodland,
    We'll dance and then feast in a dairy.
Though youngest of all in our good band,
    She is wasting away, little fairy.

She who Dwelt among the Sycamores

A Fancy

A little boy outside the sycamore wood
    Saw on the wood's edge gleam an ash-grey feather;
    A kid, held by one soft white ear for tether,
Trotted beside him in a playful mood.
A little boy inside the sycamore wood
    Followed a ringdove's ash-grey gleam of feather.
    Noon wrapt the trees in veils of violet weather,
And on tiptoe the winds a-whispering stood.
Deep in the woodland paused they, the six feet

Lapped in the lemon daffodils; a bee
In the long grass – four eyes droop low – a seat
Of moss, a maiden weaving. Singeth she:
'I am lone Lady Quietness, my sweet,
And on this loom I weave thy destiny.'

On Mr Nettleship's Picture at the Royal Hibernian Academy

Yonder the sickle of the moon sails on,
But here the Lioness licks her soft cub
Tender and fearless on her funeral pyre;
Above, saliva dripping from his jaws,
The Lion, the world's great solitary, bends
Lowly the head of his magnificence
And roars, mad with the touch of the unknown,
Not as he shakes the forest; but a cry
Low, long and musical. A dew-drop hung
Bright on a grass blade's under side, might hear,
Nor tremble to its fall. The fire sweeps round
Re-shining in his eyes. So ever moves
The flaming circle of the outer Law,
Nor heeds the old, dim protest and the cry
The orb of the most inner living heart
Gives forth. He, the Eternal, works His will.

A Legend

A drowned city is supposed to lie under the waters of Lough Gill.

The Maker of the stars and worlds
  Sat underneath the market cross,
And the old men were walking, walking,
  And little boys played pitch and toss.

'The props,' said He, 'of stars and worlds
  Are prayers of patient men and good.'
The boys, the women, and old men,
  Listening, upon their shadows stood.

A grey professor passing cried,
  'How few the mind's intemperance rule!
What shallow thoughts about deep things!
  The world grows old and plays the fool.'

The mayor came, leaning his deaf ear –
  There was some talking of the poor –
And to himself cried, 'Communist!'
  And hurried to the guard-house door.

The bishop came with open book,
  Whispering along the sunny path;
There was some talking of man's god,
  His god of stupor and of wrath.

The bishop murmured, 'Atheist!
  How sinfully the wicked scoff!'
And sent the old men on their way,
  And drove the boys and women off.

The place was empty now of people.
  A cock came by upon his toes;
An old horse looked across a fence,
  And rubbed along the rail his nose.

The Maker of the stars and worlds
 To His own house did him betake,
And on that city dropped a tear,
 And now that city is a lake.

An Old Song Re-sung*

Down by the salley gardens my love and I did meet;
She passed the salley gardens with little snow-white feet.
She bid me take love easy as the leaves grow on the tree;
But I, being young and foolish, with her would not agree.

In a field by the river my love and I did stand,
And on my leaning shoulder she laid her snow-white hand.
She bid me take life easy as the grass grows on the weirs;
But I was young and foolish, and now am full of tears.

---

* This is an attempt to reconstruct an old song from three lines imperfectly remem-
bered by an old peasant woman in the village of Ballysodare, Sligo, who often
sings them to herself.

Street Dancers

Singing in this London street
To the rhythm of their feet,
By a window's feeble light
Are two ragged children bright –
Larger sparrows of the town,
Nested 'mong the vapours brown.
Far away the starry mirth
Hangs o'er all the wooded earth.

If these merry ones should know,
Footing in the feeble glow,
Of a wide wood's leafy leisure,
Would they foot so fleet a measure?
Ah no!

Maybe now in some far lane,
Dancing on the moon's broad stain,
Watched of placid poplar trees,
Children sing in twos and threes.

Hush! hush! hush! on every lip
Lies a chubby finger-tip,
As there floats from fields afar
Clamour of the lone nightjar.

If these merry ones should know,
Footing in the feeble glow,
Other people's mirth and pleasure,
Would they foot so fleet a measure?
Ah no!

Maybe in some isle of isles,
In the south seas' azure miles,
Dance the savage children small,
Singing to their light footfall.

Hush! hush! hush! they pause and point
Where a shell, the seas anoint,
Dropping liquid rainbow light,
Rolls along the sea-sands white.

If these merry ones should know,
Footing in the feeble glow,
Other people's mirth and pleasure,
Would they foot so fleet a measure?
Ah no!

Maybe now a Bedouin's brood
Laughing goes in wildest mood,
Past the spears and palm-stems dry,
Past the camel's dreaming eye.
Hush! hush! hush! they pause them where
Bows the Bedouin's whitening hair –
Peace of youth and peace of age,
Thoughtless joys and sorrows sage.

If these merry ones should know,
Footing in the feeble glow,
Other people's mirth and pleasure,
Would they foot so fleet a measure?
Ah no!

Others know the healing earth,
Others know the starry mirth;
They will wrap them in the shroud,
Sorrow-worn, yet placid browed.
London streets have heritage
Blinder sorrows, harder wage –
Sordid sorrows of the mart,
Sorrows sapping brain and heart.

If these merry ones should know,
Footing in the feeble glow,
All the healing earth may treasure,
Would they foot so fleet a measure?
Ah no!

To an Isle in the Water

Shy one, shy one,
  Shy one of my heart,
She moves in the firelight
  Pensively apart.

She carries in the dishes,
  And lays them in a row.
To an isle in the water
  With her would I go.

She carries in the candles,
  And lights the curtained room;
Shy in the doorway
  And shy in the gloom;

And shy as a rabbit,
  Helpful and shy.
To an isle in the water
  With her would I fly.

Quatrains and Aphorisms

I

The child who chases lizards in the grass,
The sage who deep in central nature delves,
The preacher watching for the ill hour to pass –
All these are souls who fly from their dread selves.

II

Two spirit-things a man hath for his friends —
Sorrow, that gives for guerdon liberty,
And joy, the touching of whose finger lends
To lightest of all light things sanctity.

III

Long thou for nothing, neither sad nor gay;
Long thou for nothing, neither night nor day;
Not even 'I long to see thy longing over,'
To the ever-longing and mournful spirit say.

IV

The ghosts went by me with their lips apart
From death's late languor as these lines I read
On Brahma's gateway, 'They within have fed
The soul upon the ashes of the heart.'

V

This heard I where, amid the apple trees,
Wild indolence and music have no date,
'I laughed upon the lips of Sophocles,
I go as soft as folly; I am Fate.'

VI

'Around, the twitter of the lips of dust
A tossing laugh between their red abides;
With patient beauty yonder Attic bust
In the deep alcove's dimness smiles and hides.'

VII

The heart of noon folds silence and folds sleep,
For noon and midnight from each other borrow,
And Joy, in growing deeper and more deep,
Walks in the vesture of her sister Sorrow.

The Seeker

A Dramatic Poem – in Two Scenes

SCENE I

A woodland valley at evening. Around a wood fire sit three SHEPHERDS.

First Shepherd. Heavy with wool the sheep are gathered in,
And through the mansion of the spirit rove
My dreams round thoughts of plenty, as in gloom
Of desert-caves the red-eyed panthers rove
And rove unceasing round their dreadful brood.
Second Shepherd. O brother, lay thy flute upon thy lips;
It is the voice of all our hearts that laugh.
　　　[*The first* SHEPHERD *puts the flute to his lips; there comes from it a*
　　　　　　　　　　　　　　　piercing cry. He drops it.
First Shepherd. It is possessed.
Second Shepherd.　　　　A prophesying voice.
Third Shepherd. Nay, give it me, and I will sound a measure;
And unto it we'll dance upon the sward.
　　　　[*Puts it to his lips. A voice out of the flute still more mournful.*
First Shepherd. An omen!
Second Shepherd. An omen!
Third Shepherd. A creeping horror is all over me.

Enter an OLD KNIGHT. *They cast themselves down before him.*

Knight. Are all things well with you and with your sheep?
Second Shepherd. Yes, all is very well.

First Shepherd.   Whence comest thou?

Knight. Shepherds, I came this morning to your land
From threescore years of dream-led wandering
Where spice-isles nestle on the star-trod seas,
And where the polar winds and waters wrestle
In endless dark, and by the weedy marge
Of Asian rivers, rolling on in light.
But now my wandering shall be done, I know.
A voice came calling me to this your land,
Where lies the long-lost forest of the sprite,
The sullen wood. But many woods I see
Where to themselves innumerable birds
Make moan and cry.

First Shepherd. Within yon sunless valley,
Between the hornèd hills –

Knight.   Shepherds, farewell!
And peace be with you, peace and wealth of days.

Second Shepherd. Seek not that wood, for there the goblin snakes
Go up and down, and raise their heads and sing
With little voices songs of fearful things.

Third Shepherd. No shepherd foot has ever dared its depths.

First Shepherd. The very squirrel dies that enters there.

Knight. Shepherds, farewell!   [*Goes.*

Second Shepherd.   He soon will be –

First Shepherd.   Ashes
Before the wind.

Third Shepherd. Saw you his eyes a-glitter?
His body shake?

Second Shepherd. Ay, quivering as yon smoke
That from the fire is ever pouring up
Among the boughs, blue as the halcyon's wing,
Star-envious.

Third Shepherd. He was a spirit, brother.

Second Shepherd. The blessèd God was good to send us such,
To make us glad with wonder as we sat
Weary of watching round the fire at night.

A ruined palace in the forest. Away in the depth of the shadow of the pillars a motionless FIGURE.

Enter the OLD KNIGHT.

Knight. Behold, I bend before thee to the ground
Until my beard is in the twisted leaves
That with their fiery ruin fill the hall,
As words of thine through fourscore years have filled
My echoing heart. Now raise thy voice and speak!
Even from boyhood, in my father's house,
That was beside the waterfall, thy words
Abode, as banded adders in my breast.
Thou knowest this, and how from 'mid the dance
Thou called'st me forth.
                              And how thou madest me
A coward in the field; and, all men cried:
'Behold the Knight of the waterfall, whose heart
The spirits stole, and gave him in its stead
A peering hare's;' and yet I murmured not,
Knowing that thou hadst singled me with word
Of love from out a dreamless race for strife,
Through miseries unhuman ever on
To joys unhuman, and to thee – Speak! Speak!
                    [*He draws nearer to the* FIGURE. *A pause.*
Behold, I bend before thee to the ground;
Thou wilt not speak, and I with age am near
To Death. His darkness and his chill I feel.
Were all my wandering days of no avail,
Untouched of human joy or human love?
Then let me see thy face before I die.
Behold, I bend before thee to the ground!
Behold, I bend! Around my beard in drifts
Lie strewn the yellow leaves – the clotted leaves.
                    [*He gathers up the leaves and presses them to his breast.*
I'm dying! Oh, forgive me if I touch
Thy garments' hem, thou visionary one!

[*He goes close to the* FIGURE. *A sudden light bursts over it.*
A bearded witch, her sluggish head low bent
On her broad breast! Beneath her withered brows
Shine dull unmoving eyes. What thing art thou?
I sought thee not.
Figure.   Men call me Infamy.
I know not what I am.
Knight.   I sought thee not.
Figure. Lover, the voice that summoned thee was mine.
Knight. For all I gave the voice, for all my youth,
For all my joy – ah, woe!
      [*The* FIGURE *raises a mirror, in which the face and the form of the*
                              KNIGHT *are shadowed. He falls.*
Figure (*bending over him and speaking in his ear*).
        What, lover, die before our lips have met?
Knight. Again, the voice! the voice!   [*Dies.*

Island of Statues

A Fragment

Summary of Previous Scenes

Two shepherds at dawn meet before the door of the shepherdess
Naschina and sing to her in rivalry. Their voices grow louder and
louder as they try to sing each other down. At last she comes out, a
little angry. An arrow flies across the scene. The two shepherds fly,
being full of Arcadian timidity. Almintor, who is loved by Naschina,
comes in, having shot the arrow at a heron. Naschina receives him
angrily. 'No one in Arcadia is courageous,' she says. Others, to prove
their love, go upon some far and dangerous quest. They but bring
Arcadian gifts, small birds and beasts. She goes again angrily into her
cottage. Almintor seeks the enchanted island, to find for her the
mysterious flower, guarded there by the Enchantress and her spirits.
He is led thither by a voice singing in a valley. The island is full of

flowers and of people turned into stone. They chose the wrong flower. He also chooses wrong, and is turned into stone. Naschina resolves to seek him disguised as a shepherd. On her way she meets with the two shepherds of Scene I; they do not recognize her, but like to be near her. They tell her they love one maid; she answers, if that be so, they must clearly settle it by combat. She, not believing they will do so, passes on and comes to the edge of the lake in which is the enchanted island, and is carried over in a boat with wings. The shepherds also come to the edge of the lake. They fight fiercely, made courageous by love. One is killed. The scene quoted gives the adventures of Naschina on the island.

SCENE III

The Island. Flowers of manifold colour are knee-deep before a gate of brass, above which, in a citron-tinctured sky, glimmer a few stars. At intervals come mournful blasts from the horns among the flowers.

First Voice. What do you weave so fair and bright?
Second Voice. The cloak I weave of Sorrow.
　　Oh, lovely to see in all men's sight
Shall be the cloak of Sorrow,
　　In all men's sight.
Third Voice. What do you build with sails for flight?
Fourth Voice. A boat I build for Sorrow.
　　Oh, swift on the seas all day and night
Saileth the rover Sorrow,
　　All day and night.
Fifth Voice. What do you weave with wool so white?
Sixth Voice. The sandals these of Sorrow.
　　Soundless shall be the footfall light,
In each man's ears, of Sorrow,
　　Sudden and light.

NASCHINA, *disguised as a shepherd-boy, enters with the* ENCHANTRESS, *the beautiful familiar of the Isle.*

Naschina. What are the voices that in flowery ways

Have clothed their tongues with song of songless days?
Enchantress They are the flowers' guardian sprites;
   With streaming hair as wandering lights
   They passed a-tiptoe everywhere,
   And never heard of grief or care
   Until this morn. The sky with wrack
   Was banded as an adder's back,
   And they were sitting round a pool.
   At their feet the waves in rings
   Gently shook their moth-like wings;
   For there came an air-breath cool
   From the ever-moving pinions
   Of the happy flower minions.
   But a sudden melancholy
   Filled them as they sat together;
   Now their songs are mournful wholly
   As they go with drooping feather.
Naschina. O Lady, thou whose vesiture of green
Is rolled as verdant smoke! O thou whose face
Is worn as though with fire! O goblin queen,
Lead me, I pray thee, to the statued place!
Enchantress. Fair youth, along a wandering way
   I've led thee here, and as a wheel
   We turned around the place alway,
   Lest on thine heart the stony seal
   As on those other hearts were laid.
   Behold the brazen-gated glade!
  [She partially opens the brazen gates. The statues are seen within.
    Some are bending, with their hands among the flowers;
     others are holding withered flowers.
Naschina. Oh, let me pass! The spells from off the heart
Of my sad hunter-friend will all depart
If on his lips the enchanted flower be laid.
Oh, let me pass!
     [Leaning with an arm upon each gate.
Enchantress. That flower none
   Who seek may find, save only one,
   A shepherdess long years foretold;
   And even she shall never hold

The flower, save some thing be found
To die for her in air or ground.
And none there is; if such there were,
E'en then, before her shepherd hair
Had left the island breeze, my lore
Had driven her forth, for evermore
To wander by the bubbling shore,
Laughter-lipped, but for her brain
A guerdon of deep-rooted pain,
And in her eyes a lightless stare;
For, if severed from the root
The enchanted flower were;
From my wizard island lair,
And the happy wingèd day,
I, as music that grows mute
On a girl's forgotten lute,
Pass away –
Naschina. Your eyes are all aflash. She is not here.
Enchantress. I'd kill her if she were. Nay, do not fear!
With you I am all gentleness; in truth,
There's little I'd refuse thee, dearest youth.
Naschina. It is my whim! bid some attendant sprite
Of thine cry over wold and water white,
That one shall die, unless one die for her.
'Tis but to see if anything will stir
For such a call. Let the wild word be cried
As though she whom you fear had crossed the wide
Swift lake.
Enchantress. A very little thing that is
And shall be done, if you will deign to kiss
My lips, fair youth.
Naschina.   It shall be as you ask.
Enchantress. Forth! forth! O spirits, ye have heard your task!
Voices. We are gone!
Enchantress (*sitting down by* NASCHINA). Fair shepherd, as we
                                        wandered hither,
My words were all: 'Here no loves wane and wither,
Where dream-fed passion is and peace encloses,
Where revel of foxglove is and revel of roses.'

My words were all: 'O whither, whither, whither
Wilt roam away from this rich island rest?'
I bid thee stay, renouncing thy mad quest,
But thou wouldst not, for then thou wert unblest
And stony-hearted; now thou hast grown kind,
And thou wilt stay. All thought of what they find
In the far world will vanish from thy mind,
Till thou rememberest only how the sea
Has fenced us round for all eternity.
But why art thou so silent? Didst thou hear
I laughed?
Naschina. And why is that a thing so dear?
Enchantress. From thee I snatched it; e'en the fay that trips
At morn, and with her feet each cobweb rends,
Laughs not. It dwells alone on mortal lips:
Thou'lt teach me laughing, and I'll teach thee peace
Here where laburnum hangs her golden fleece;
For peace and laughter have been seldom friends.
But, for a boy, how long thine hair has grown!
Long citron coils that hang around thee, blown
In shadowy dimness. To be fair as thee
I'd give my fairy fleetness, though I be
Far fleeter than the million-footed sea.
A Voice. By wood antique, by wave and waste,
Where cypress is and oozy pine,
    Did I on quivering pinions haste,
And all was quiet round me spread,
As quiet as the clay-cold dead.
I cried the thing you bade me cry.
    An owl, who in an alder tree
Had hooted for an hundred years,
    Upraised his voice, and hooted me.
E'en though his wings were plumeless stumps,
    And all his veins had near run dry,
Forth from the hollow alder trunk
    He hooted as I wandered by.
And so with wolf and boar, and steer.
    And one alone of all would hark,
A man who by a dead man stood.

A starlit rapier, half blood–dark,
Was broken in his quivering hand.
　As blossoms, when the winds of March
Hold festival across the land,
He shrank before my voice, and stood
　Low bowed and dumb upon the sand.
A foolish word thou gavest me!
　For each within himself hath all;
The world within his folded heart –
　His temple and his banquet hall;
And who will throw his mansion down
　Thus for another's bugle call!
Enchantress. But why this whim of thine? A strange unrest,
Alien as cuckoo in a robin's nest,
Is in thy face, and lip together pressed;
And why so silent? I would have thee speak.
Soon wilt thou smile, for here the winds are weak
As moths with broken wings, and as we sit
The heavens all star throbbing are alit.
Naschina. But art thou happy?
Enchantress. Let me gaze on thee,
At arm's length thus; till dumb eternity
Has rolled away the stars and dried the sea
I could gaze, gaze upon thine eyes of grey;
Gaze on till ragged Time himself decay.
Ah! you are weeping; here should all grief cease.
Naschina. But art thou happy?
Enchantress. 　　　　　　　Youth, I am at peace.
Naschina. But art thou happy?
Enchantress. 　　　　　　　Those grey eyes of thine,
Have they ne'er seen the eyes of lynx or kine,
Or aught remote; or hast thou never heard
'Mid babbling leaves a wandering song-rapt bird
Going the forest through, with flutings weak;
Or hast thou never seen, with visage meek,
A hoary hunter leaning on his bow,
To watch thee pass? Yet deeper than men know
These are at peace.
A Voice. Sad lady, cease!

I rose, I rose
    From the dim wood's foundation –
I rose, I rose
    Where in white exultation
The long lily blows,
And the wan wave that lingers
    From flood-time encloses
With infantine fingers
    The roots of the roses.
Now here I come winging;
    I there had been keeping
    A mouse from his sleeping,
With shouting and singing.
Enchantress. How sped thy quest? This prelude we'll not hear it.
I' faith thou ever wast a wordy spirit!
The Voice. A wriggling thing on the white lake moved,
    As the canker-worm on a milk-white rose;
And down I came as a falcon swoops
    When his sinewy wings together close.
I 'lit by the thing, 'twas a shepherd-boy,
    Who, swimming, sought the island lone;
Within his clenchèd teeth a sword.
    I heard the dreadful monotone
The water-serpent sings his heart
Before a death. O'er wave and bank
    I cried the words you bid me cry.
The shepherd raised his arms and sank,
    His rueful spirit fluttered by.
Naschina (aside). I must bestir myself. Both dead for me!
Both dead! – No time for thinking.
(Aloud)   I am she.
That shepherdess: arise, and bring to me,
In silence, that famed flower of wizardry,
For I am mightier now by far than thee,
And faded now is all thy wondrous art.
                    [*The* ENCHANTRESS *points to a cleft in a rock.*
I see within a cloven rock dispart
A scarlet bloom. Why raisest thou, pale one,
O famous dying minion of the sun,

Thy flickering hand? What mean the lights that rise
As light of triumph in thy goblin eyes –
In thy wan face?
Enchantress.   Hear, daughter of the days.
Behold the loving loveless flower of lone ways,
Well-nigh immortal in this charmèd clime;
Thou shalt outlive thine amorous happy time,
And dead as are the lovers of old rhyme
Shall be the hunter-lover of thy youth.
Yet evermore, through all thy days of ruth,
Shall grow thy beauty and thy dreamless truth;
As a hurt leopard fills with ceaseless moan
And aimless wanderings the woodlands lone,
Thy soul shall be, though pitiless and bright
It is, yet shall it fail thee day and night
Beneath the burden of the infinite,
In those fair years, O daughter of the days.
And when thou hast these things for ages felt,
The red squirrel shall rear her young where thou hast dwelt –
Ah, woe is me! I go from sun and shade,
And the joy of the streams where long-limbed herons wade;
And never any more the wide-eyed bands
Of the pied panther-kittens from my hands
Shall feed. I shall not in the evenings hear
Again the woodland laughter, and the clear
Wild cries, grown sweet with lulls and lingerings long.
I fade, and shall not see the mornings wake,
A-fluttering the painted populace of lake
And sedgy stream, and in each babbling brake
And hollow lulling the young winds with song.
I dream! – I cannot die! – not die! No! no!
I hurl away these all unfaery fears.
Have I not seen a thousand seasons ebb and flow
The tide of stars? Have I not seen a thousand years
The summers fling their scents? Ah, subtile and slow,
The warmth of life is chilling, and the shadows grow
More dark beneath the poplars, where yon owl
Lies torn and rotting. The fierce kestrel birds
Slew thee, poor sibyl: comrades thou and I;

For ah, our lives were but two starry words
Shouted a moment 'tween the earth and sky.
Oh, death is horrible! and foul, foul, foul!
Naschina. I know not of the things you speak. But what
Of him on yonder brazen-gated spot,
By thee spell-bound?
Enchantress.   Thou shalt know more:
Meeting long hence the phantom herdsman, king
Of the dread woods; along their russet floor
His sleuth-hounds follow every fairy thing.

                              [*Turns to go.* NASCHINA *tries to prevent her.*
Before I am too weak, oh let me fly,
Fierce mortal, and crouched low beside the lake
In a far stillness of the island die.   [*Goes.*
Naschina (following). Will he have happiness? Great sobs her being
shake.
Voices (sing).

A man has the fields of heaven,
    But soulless a fairy dies,
As a leaf that is old, and withered, and cold,
    When the wintry vapours rise.

Soon shall our wings be stilled,
    And our laughter over and done:
So let us dance where the yellow lance
    Of the barley shoots in the sun.

So let us dance on the fringèd waves
    And shout at the wisest owls
In their downy caps, and startle the naps
    Of the dreaming water-fowls,

And fight for the black sloe-berries,
    For soulless a fairy dies,
As a leaf that is old, and withered, and cold,
    When the wintry vapours rise.

Naschina. I plucked her backwards by her dress of green.
To question her – oh no, I did not fear,
Because St Joseph's image hangeth here
Upon my necklace. But the goblin queen
Faded and vanished: nothing now is seen,
Saving a green frog dead upon the grass.
As figures moving mirrored in a glass,
The singing shepherds, too, have passed away.
O Arcady, O Arcady, this day
A deal of evil and of change hath crossed
Thy peace. Ah, now I'll wake these sleepers, lost
And woe-begone. For them no evil day!

        [*Throws open the brazen gates.*

(*To* ALMINTOR) O wake! wake! wake! for soft as a bee sips
The fairy flower lies upon thy lips.
Almintor. I slept, 'twas sultry, and scarce circling shook
The falling hawthorn bloom. By mere and brook
The otters dreaming lay. Naschina!
Naschina.   Ay!
Behold the hapless sleepers standing by.
I will dissolve away the faeries' guile;
So be thou still, dear heart, a little while!
(*To the* SECOND SLEEPER) Old warrior, wake! for soft as a bee sips
The fairy blossom lies upon thy lips.
Sleeper. Have I slept long?
Naschina.   Long years.
The Sleeper.   With hungry heart
Doth still the Wanderer rove? With all his ships
I saw him from sad Dido's shores depart,
Enamoured of the waves' impetuous lips.
Naschina. Those twain are dust. Wake! Light as a bee sips
The fairy blossom lies upon thy lips;
Seafarer, wake!
Third Sleeper. Was my sleep long?
Naschina.   Long years.
Third Sleeper. A rover I who come from where men's ears
Love storm and stained with mist the new moon's flare.
Doth still the man whom each stern rover fears –

The austere Arthur – rule from Uther's chair?
Naschina. He is long dead.
        Wake! soft as a bee sips
The goblin flower lieth on thy lips.
Fourth Sleeper. Was my sleep long, O youth?
Naschina.   Long, long and deep.
The Sleeper. As here I came I saw god Pan. He played
An oaten pipe unto a listening faun,
Whose insolent eyes unused to tears would weep.
Doth he still dwell within the woody shade,
And rule the shadows of the eve and dawn?
Naschina. Nay, he is gone. Wake! wake! as a bee sips
The fairy blossom broods upon thy lips.
Sleeper, awake!
Fifth Sleeper. How long my sleep?
Naschina.   Unnumbered
The years of goblin sleep.
The Sleeper. Ah! while I slumbered,
How have the years in Troia flown away?
Are still the Achaians' tented chiefs at bay?
Where rise the walls majestical above,
There dwells a little fair-haired maid I love.
The Sleepers all together. She is long ages dust.
The Sleeper.   Ah, woe is me!
First Sleeper. Youth, here will we abide, and be thou king
Of this lake-nurtured isle!
Naschina.   Let thy king be
Yon archer, he who hath the halcyon's wing
As flaming minstrel-word upon his crest.
All the Sleepers. Clear-browed Arcadian, thou shalt be our king!
Naschina. O, my Almintor, noble was thy quest;
Yea, noble and most knightly hath it been.
All the Sleepers. Clear-browed Arcadian, thou shalt be our king!
Almintor. Until we die within the charmèd ring
Of these star-shuddering skies, you are the queen.

 [*The rising moon casts the shadows of* ALMINTOR *and the*
 SLEEPERS *far across the grass. Close by* ALMINTOR'S *side,*
 NASCHINA *is standing, shadowless.*

LEGENDS AND LYRICS
(1892)

The souls are threshed and the stars threshed from their husks.
(From an unpublished MS by William Blake)

To the Rose upon the Rood of Time

Red Rose, proud Rose, sad Rose of all my days,
Come near me, while I sing the ancient ways –
Cuchullin battling with the bitter tide;
The druid, grey, wood nurtured, quiet eyed,
Who cast round Fergus dreams and ruin untold;
And thine own sadness, whereof stars grown old
In dancing silver sandaled on the sea,
Sing in their high and lonely melody.
Come near, that no more blinded by man's fate,
I find under the boughs of love and hate,
In all poor foolish things that live a day,
Eternal Beauty wandering on her way.

Come near, come near, come near – Ah, leave me still
A little space for the rose-breath to fill,
Lest I no more hear common things that crave,
The weak worm hiding down in its small cave –
The field mouse running by me in the grass,
And heavy mortal hopes that toil and pass,
But seek alone to hear the strange things said
By God to the bright hearts of those long dead,
And learn to chant a tongue men do not know.
Come near – I would, before my time to go,
Sing of old Eri and the ancient ways,
Red Rose, proud Rose, sad Rose of all my days.

Fergus and the Druid

FERGUS

The whole day have I followed in the rocks,
And you have changed and flowed from shape to shape.
First as a raven on whose ancient wings
Scarcely a feather lingered, then you seemed
A weasel moving on from stone to stone,
And now at last you take on human shape –
A thin grey man half lost in gathering night.

DRUID

What would you, king of the proud Red Branch kings?

FERGUS

This would I say, most wise of living souls:
Young subtle Concobar sat close by me
When I gave judgment, and his words were wise,
And what to me was burden without end,
To him seemed easy, so I laid the crown
Upon his head to cast away my care.

DRUID

What would you, king of the proud Red Branch kings?

FERGUS

I feast amid my people on the hill,
And pace the woods, and drive my chariot wheels
In the white border of the murmuring sea;
And still I feel the crown upon my head.

DRUID

What would you?

FERGUS

I would be no more a king,
But learn the dreaming wisdom that is yours.

DRUID

Look on my thin grey hair and hollow cheeks,
And on these hands that may not lift the sword,
This body trembling like a wind-blown reed.
No maiden loves me, no man seeks my help,
Because I be not of the things I dream.

FERGUS

A wild and foolish labourer is a king,
To do and do and do and never dream.

DRUID

Take, if you must, this little bag of dreams,
Unloose the cord and they will wrap you round.

FERGUS (*having unloosed the cord*)

I see my life go dripping like a stream
From change to change; I have been many things –
A green drop in the surge, a gleam of light
Upon a sword, a fir-tree on a hill,
An old slave grinding at a heavy quern,
A king sitting upon a chair of gold,
And all these things were wonderful and great;
But now I have grown nothing, being all,
And the whole world weighs down upon my heart –
Ah! Druid, Druid, how great webs of sorrow
Lay hidden in the small slate-coloured bag!

The Rose of the World

Who dreamed that beauty passes like a dream?
  For these red lips with all their mournful pride,
  Mournful that no new wonder may betide,
Troy passed away in one high funeral gleam,
  And Usna's children died.

We and the labouring world are passing by: −
  Amid men's souls that day by day gives place,
  More fleeting than the sea's foam fickle face,
Under the passing stars, foam of the sky,
  Lives on this lonely face.

Bow down archangels in your dim abode:
  Before ye were or any hearts to beat,
  Weary and kind one stood beside His seat,
He made the world to be a grassy road
  Before her wandering feet.

The Peace of the Rose

If Michael, leader of God's host
  When Heaven and Hell are met,
Looked down on you from Heaven's door-post,
  He would his deeds forget.

Brooding no more upon God's wars
  In His Divine homestead,
He would go weave out of the stars
  A chaplet for your head;

And all folk seeing him bow down,
  And white stars tell your praise,
Would come at last to God's great town,
  Led on by gentle ways;

And God would bid His warfare cease,
  Saying all things were well,
And softly make a rosy peace,
  A peace of Heaven with Hell.

The Death of Cuchullin

A man came slowly from the setting sun,
To Emer of Borda, in her clay-piled dun,
And found her dyeing cloth with subtle care,
And said, casting aside his draggled hair,
'I am Aileel, the swineherd, whom you bid
Go dwell upon the sea cliffs, vapour hid,
But now my years of watching are no more.'

Then Emer cast the web upon the floor,
And stretching out her arms, red with the dye,
Parted her lips with a loud sudden cry.

Looking on her, Aileel, the swineherd, said
'Not any god alive nor mortal dead,
Has slain so mighty armies, so great kings,
Nor won the gold that now Cuchullin brings.'

'Why do you tremble thus from feet to crown?'
Aileel, the swineherd, wept and cast him down
Upon the web-heaped floor, and thus his word,
'With him is one sweet throated like a bird,
And lovelier than the moon upon the sea;
He made for her an army cease to be.'

'Who bade you tell these things upon my floor?'
Then to her servants, 'Beat him from the door
With thongs of leather.' As she spake it was;
And where her son, Finmole, on the smooth grass
Was driving cattle came she with swift feet,
And cried out to him, 'Son, it is not meet
That you stay idling here with flocks and herds.'

Long have I waited mother for those words,
But wherefore now?'
              'There is a man to die,
You have the heaviest arm under the sky.'

'My father,' made he smiling answer then,
'Still treads the world amid his armed men.'

'Nay, you are taller than Cuchullin, son.'
'He is the mightiest man in ship or dun.'

'Nay, he is old and sad with many wars,
And weary of the crash of battle cars.'

'I only ask what way my journey lies,
For God who made you bitter made you wise.'

'The Red Branch kings a tireless banquet keep,
Where the sun falls into the Western deep.
Go there and dwell on the green forest rim,
But tell alone your name and house to him
Whose blade compels, and bid them send you one
Who has a like vow from their triple dun.'

Between the lavish shelter of a wood
And the grey tide, the Red Branch multitude
Feasted, and with them old Cuchullin dwelt,
And his young dear one close beside him knelt,
And gazed upon the wisdom of his eyes,
More mournful than the depth of starry skies,
And pondered on the wonder of his days,
And all around the harp string told his praise,

And Concobar, the Red Branch king of kings,
With his own fingers touched the brazen strings.

At last Cuchullin spake, 'A young man strays
Driving the deer along the woody ways.
I often hear him singing to and fro,
I often hear the sweet sound of his bow.
Seek out what man he is.'
                              One went and came.
'He bade me let all know he gives his name
At the sword point and bade me bring him one,
Who had a like vow from our triple dun.'

'I only of the Red Branch hosted now,'
Cuchullin cried, 'have made and keep that vow.'

After short fighting in the leafy shade,
He spake to the young man, 'Is there no maid
Who loves you, no white arms to wrap you round,
Or do you long for the dim sleepy ground,
That you come here to meet this ancient sword?'

'God only sees what doom for me lies stored.'

'Your head a while seemed like a woman's head
That I loved once.'
                        Again the fighting sped,
But now the war rage in Cuchullin woke,
And through the other's shield his long blade broke,
And pierced him.
                       'Speak before your breath is done.'

'I am Finmole, mighty Cuchullin's son.'

'I put you from your pain. I can no more.'

While day its burden on to evening bore,
With head bowed on his knees Cuchullin staid,
Then Concobar sent that sweet throated maid

And she to win him, his grey hair caressed –
In vain her arms, in vain her soft white breast.
Then Concobar, the subtlest of all men,
Sent for his druids twenty score and ten,
And cried, 'Cuchullin will dwell there and brood,
For three days more in dreadful quietude,
And then arise, and raving slay us all.
Go, cast on him delusions magical,
That he may fight the waves of the loud sea.'
Near to Cuchullin, round a quicken tree,
The Druids chanted, swaying in their hands
Tall wands of alder and white quicken wands.

In three days time he stood up with a moan,
And he went down to the long sands alone,
For four days warred he with the bitter tide,
And the waves flowed above him, and he died.

The White Birds

I would that we were, my beloved, white birds on the foam of the
sea,
We tire of the flame of the meteor, before it can pass by and flee;
And the flame of the blue star of twilight, hung low on the rim of
the sky,
Has awaked in our hearts, my beloved, a sadness that never may die.

A weariness comes from those dreamers, dew dabbled, the lily and
rose,
Ah, dream not of them, my beloved, the flame of the meteor that
goes,
Or the flame of the blue star that lingers hung low in the fall of the
dew:
For I would we were changed to white birds on the wandering
foam – I and you.

I am haunted by numberless islands, and many a Danaan shore,
Where Time would surely forget us, and Sorrow come near us no
more,
Soon far from the rose and the lily, and fret of the flames would we
be,
Were we only white birds, my beloved, buoyed out on the foam
of the sea.

Father Gilligan

The old priest Peter Gilligan
    Was weary night and day,
For half his flock were in their beds
    Or under green sods lay.

Once, while he nodded on a chair,
    At the moth-hour of eve,
Another poor man sent for him,
    And he began to grieve.

'I have no rest, nor joy, nor peace,
    For people die and die;'
And after cried he, 'God forgive!
    My body spake, not I!'

And then, half-lying on the chair,
    He knelt, prayed, fell asleep;
And the moth-hour went from the fields,
    And stars began to peep.

They slowly into millions grew,
    And leaves shook in the wind;
And God covered the world with shade,
    And whispered to mankind.

Upon the time of sparrow chirp
  When the moths came once more,
The old priest Peter Gilligan
  Stood upright on the floor.

'Mavrone, mavrone! the man has died,
  While I slept on the chair';
He roused his horse out of its sleep,
  And rode with little care.

He rode now as he never rode,
  By rocky lane and fen;
The sick man's wife opened the door:
  'Father! you come again!'

'And is the poor man dead?' he cried.
  'He died an hour ago.'
The old priest Peter Gilligan
  In grief swayed to and fro.

'When you were gone he turned and died,
  As merry as a bird.'
The old priest Peter Gilligan
  He knelt him at that word.

'He who hath made the night of stars
  For souls who tire and bleed
Sent one of His great angels down
  To help me in my need.

'He who is wrapped in purple robes,
  With planets in his care,
Had pity on the least of things
  Asleep upon a chair.'

Father O'Hart

Good Father John O'Hart
   In penal days rode out
To a shoneen who had free lands
   And his own snipe and trout.

In trust took he John's lands —
   Sleiveens were all his race —
And he gave them as dowers to his daughters,
   And they married beyond their place.

But Father John went up,
   And Father John went down;
And he wore small holes in his shoes,
   And he wore large holes in his gown.

All loved him, only the shoneen,
   Whom the devils have by the hair,
From the wives, and the cats, and the children,
   To the birds in the white of the air.

The birds, for he opened their cages
   As he went up and down;
And he said with a smile, 'Have peace now,'
   And he went his way with a frown.

But if when any one died
   Came keeners hoarser than rooks,
He bade them give over their keening,
   For he was a man of books.

And these were the works of John,
   When weeping score by score,
People came into Coloony,
   For he'd died at ninety-four.

There was no human keening;
    The birds from Knocknarea
And the world round Knocknashee
    Came keening in that day.

The young birds and old birds
    Came flying, heavy, and sad,
Keening in from Tiraragh,
    Keening from Ballinafad;

Keening from Innismurry,
    Nor stayed for bite or sup;
This way were all reproved
    Who dig old customs up.

When You Are Old

When you are old and grey and full of sleep,
    And nodding by the fire, take down this book
    And slowly read and dream of the soft look
Your eyes had once, and of their shadows deep.

How many loved your moments of glad grace,
    And loved your beauty with love false or true,
    But one man loved the pilgrim soul in you,
And loved the sorrows of your changing face.

And bending down beside the glowing bars
    Murmur, a little sad, 'From us fled Love.
    He paced upon the mountains far above,
And hid his face amid a crowd of stars.'

The Sorrow of Love

The quarrel of the sparrows in the eaves,
   The full round moon and the star-laden sky,
And the loud song of the ever-singing leaves
   Had hid away earth's old and weary cry.

And then you came with those red mournful lips,
   And with you came the whole of the world's tears,
And all the sorrows of her labouring ships,
   And all the burden of her myriad years.

And now the sparrows warring in the eaves,
   The crumbling moon, the white stars in the sky,
And the loud chanting of the unquiet leaves,
   Are shaken with earth's old and weary cry.

The Ballad of the Old Foxhunter

'Now lay me in a cushioned chair
   And carry me ye four,
With cushions here and cushions there,
   To see the world once more.

'And some one from the stable bring
   My Dermot dear and brown,
And lead him gently in a ring,
   And gently up and down.

'Now leave the chair upon the grass,
   Bring hound and huntsman here,
And I on this strange road will pass
   Filled full of ancient cheer.'

His eyelids droop, his head falls low,
　　His old eyes cloud with dreams;
The sun upon all things that grow,
　　Pours round in sleepy streams.

Brown Dermot treads upon the lawn,
　　And to the armchair goes,
And now the old man's dreams are gone,
　　He smooths the long brown nose.

And now moves many a pleasant tongue,
　　Upon his wasted hands,
For leading aged hounds and young
　　The huntsman near him stands.

'Now huntsman Rody, blow thy horn,
　　And make the hills reply.'
The huntsman loosens on the morn,
　　A gay and wandering cry.

A fire is in the old man's eyes,
　　His fingers move and sway,
And when the wandering music dies,
　　They hear him feebly say,

'Now huntsman Rody, blow thy horn,
　　And make the hills reply.'
'I cannot blow upon my horn,
　　I can but weep and sigh.'

The servants round his cushioned place
　　Are with new sorrow wrung;
And hounds are gazing on his face,
　　The old hounds and the young.

'Now huntsman Rody, blow thy horn – '
　　Die off the feeble sounds:
And gazing on his visage worn,
　　Are old and puppy hounds;

The oldest hound with mournful din,
    Lifts slow his wintry head: –
The servants bear the body in –
    The hounds keen for the dead.

A Fairy Song

*Sung by the 'Good People' over the outlaw Michael Dwyer and his bride, who
had escaped into the mountains.*

We who are old, old and gay,
    O so old,
Thousands of years, thousands of years,
    If all were told:

Give to these children new from the world
    Silence and love,
And the long dew-dropping hours of the night
    And the stars above:

Give to these children new from the world
    Rest far from men.
Is anything better, anything better?
    Tell it us then:

Us who are old, old and gay,
    O so old,
Thousands of years, thousands of years,
    If all were told.

The Pity of Love

A pity beyond all telling,
  Is hid in the heart of love;
The folk who are buying and selling,
  The stars of God where they move,
The mouse-grey waters on flowing,
  The clouds on their journey above,
And the cold wet winds ever blowing,
  All threaten the head that I love.

The Lake Isle of Innisfree

I will arise and go now, and go to Innisfree,
  And a small cabin build there, of clay and wattles made;
Nine bean rows will I have there, a hive for the honey bee,
  And live alone in the bee-loud glade.

And I shall have some peace there, for peace comes dropping slow,
  Dropping from the veils of the morning to where the cricket sings;
There midnight's all a glimmer, and noon a purple glow,
  And evening full of the linnet's wings.

I will arise and go now, for always night and day
  I hear lake water lapping with low sounds by the shore;
While I stand on the roadway or on the pavements gray,
  I hear it in the deep heart's core.

A Cradle Song

'Coth yani me von gilli beg,
'N heur ve thu more a creena.'

The angels are bending
    Above your white bed,
They weary of tending
    The souls of the dead.

God smiles in high heaven
    To see you so good,
The old planets seven
    Grow gay with his mood.

I kiss you and kiss you,
    With arms round my own,
Ah, how shall I miss you,
    When, dear, you have grown.

The Man who Dreamed of Fairyland

I

He stood among a crowd at Drumahair,
    His heart hung all upon a silken dress,
    And he had known at last some tenderness
Before earth made of him her sleepy care;
But when a man poured fish into a pile,
    It seemed they raised their little silver heads,
    And sang how day a Druid twilight sheds
Upon a dim, green, well-beloved isle,
Where people love beside star-laden seas;
    How Time may never mar their fairy vows
    Under the woven roofs of quicken boughs; —
The singing shook him out of his new ease.

II

As he went by the sands of Lisadill,
  His mind ran all on money cares and fears,
  And he had known at last some prudent years
Before they heaped his grave under the hill;
But while he passed before a plashy place,
  A lug-worm with its gray and muddy mouth
  Sang how somewhere to north or east or south
There dwelt a gay, exulting, gentle race;
And how beneath those three times blessed skies
  A Danaan fruitage makes a shower of moons
  And as it falls awakens leafy tunes; –
And at that singing he was no more wise.

III

He mused beside the well of Scanavin,
  He mused upon his mockers. Without fail
  His sudden vengeance were a country tale
Now that deep earth has drunk his body in
But one small knot-grass growing by the rim
  Told where – ah, little, all-unneeded voice! –
  Old Silence bids a lonely folk rejoice,
And chaplet their calm brows with leafage dim,
And how, when fades the sea-strewn rose of day,
  A gentle feeling wraps them like a fleece,
  And all their trouble dies into its peace; –
The tale drove his fine angry mood away.

IV

He slept under the hill of Lugnagall,
  And might have known at last unhaunted sleep
  Under that cold and vapour-turbaned steep,
Now that old earth had taken man and all:

Were not the worms that spired about his bones
   A-telling with their low and reedy cry,
   Of how God leans His hands out of the sky,
To bless that isle with honey in His tones,
That none may feel the power of squall and wave,
   And no one any leaf-crowned dancer miss
   Until He burn up Nature with a kiss; –
The man has found no comfort in the grave.

Dedication of 'Irish Tales'

There was a green branch hung with many a bell
   When her own people ruled in wave-worn Eri,
   And from its murmuring greenness, calm of faery,
– A Druid kindness – on all hearers fell.

It charmed away the merchant from his guile,
   And turned the farmer's memory from his cattle,
   And hushed in sleep the roaring ranks of battle,
For all who heard it dreamed a little while.

Ah, Exiles wandering over many seas,
   Spinning at all times Eri's good to-morrow,
   Ah, world-wide Nation, always growing Sorrow,
I also bear a bell branch full of ease.

I tore it from green boughs winds tossed and hurled,
   Green boughs of tossing always, weary, weary,
   I tore it from the green boughs of old Eri,
The willow of the many-sorrowed world.

Ah, Exiles, wandering over many lands,
   My bell branch murmurs: the gay bells bring laughter,
   Leaping to shake a cobweb from the rafter;
The sad bells bow the forehead on the hands.

A honied ringing, under the new skies
  They bring you memories of old village faces,
  Cabins gone now, old well-sides, old dear places,
And men who loved the cause that never dies.

The Lamentation of the Old Pensioner

I had a chair at every hearth,
  When no one turned to see,
With 'look at that old fellow there,
  And who may he be?'
And therefore do I wander on,
  And the fret lies on me.

The road-side trees keep murmuring.
  Ah, wherefore murmur ye,
As in the old days long gone by,
  Green oak and poplar tree?
The well-known faces are all gone
  And the fret lies on me.

When You Are Sad

When you are sad,
  The mother of the stars weeps too,
And all her starlight is with sorrow mad,
  And tears of fire fall gently in the dew.

When you are sad,
　　The mother of the wind mourns too,
And her old wind that no mirth ever had,
　　Wanders and wails before my heart most true.

When you are sad,
　　The mother of the wave sighs too,
And her dim wave bids man be no more glad,
　　And then the whole world's trouble weeps with you.

The Two Trees

Beloved, gaze in thine own heart,
　　The holy tree is growing there;
From joy the holy branches start,
　　And all the trembling flowers they bear.
The changing colours of its fruit
　　Have dowered the stars with merry light;
The surety of its hidden root,
　　Has planted quiet in the night;
The shaking of its leafy head,
　　Has given the waves their melody,
And made my lips and music wed,
　　Murmuring a wizard song for thee.
There, through bewildered branches, go
　　Winged Loves borne on in gentle strife,
Tossing and tossing to and fro
　　The flaming circle of our life.
When looking on their shaken hair,
　　And dreaming how they dance and dart,
Thine eyes grow full of tender care: –
　　Beloved gaze in thine own heart.

Gaze no more in the bitter glass
     The demons with their subtle guile
Lift up before us when they pass,
     Or only gaze a little while;
For there a fatal image grows,
     With broken boughs and blackened leaves
And roots half hidden under snows
     Driven by a storm that ever grieves.
For all things turn to barrenness
     In the dim glass the demons hold –
The glass of outer weariness,
     Made when God slept in times of old.
There, through the broken branches, go
     The ravens of unresting thought;
Peering and flying to and fro,
     To see men's souls bartered and bought.
When they are heard upon the wind,
     And when they shake their wings – alas!
Thy tender eyes grow all unkind: –
     Gaze no more in the bitter glass.

They Went Forth to the Battle, But They Always Fell

Rose of all Roses, Rose of all the World,
The tall thought-woven sails that flap unfurled
Above the tide of hours, rise on the air,
And God's bell buoyed to be the waters' care,
And pressing on, or lingering slow with fear,
The throngs with blown wet hair are gathering near.
'Turn if ye may,' I call out to each one,
'From the grey ships and battles never won.
Danger no refuge holds, and war no peace,
For him who hears Love sing and never cease,
Besides her clean swept hearth, her quiet shade;
But gather all for whom no Love hath made
A woven silence, or but came to cast
A song into the air, and singing past
To smile upon her stars; and gather you,
Who have sought more than is in rain or dew,
Or in the sun and moon, or on the earth,
Or sighs amid the wandering, starry mirth,
Or comes in laughter from the sea's sad lips,
And wage God's battles in the long grey ships.
The sad, the lonely, the insatiable,
To these Old Night shall all her mystery tell,
God's bell has claimed them by the little cry
Of their sad hearts, that may not live nor die.'

Rose of all Roses, Rose of all the World,
You, too, have come where the dim tides are hurled
Upon the wharves of sorrow, and heard ring
The bell that calls us on – the sweet far thing.
Beauty grown sad with its eternity,
Made you of us and of the dim grey sea.
Our long ships loose thought-woven sails and wait,
For God has bid them share an equal fate;
And when at last defeated in His wars,
They have gone down under the same white stars,
We shall no longer hear the little cry
Of our sad hearts, that may not live nor die.

An Epitaph

I dreamed that one had died in a strange place
    Near no accustomed hand,
And they had nailed the boards above her face,
    The peasants of that land,
And, wondering, planted by her solitude
    A cypress and a yew.
I came and wrote upon a cross of wood
    – Man had no more to do –
'She was more beautiful than thy first love
    This lady by the trees,'
And gazed upon the mournful stars above
    And heard the mournful breeze.

Apologia Addressed to Ireland in the Coming Days

Know that I would accounted be
True brother of that company
Who sang to sweeten Ireland's wrong,
Ballad and story, rann and song;
Nor be I any less of them,
Because the red rose bordered hem
Of her whose history began
Before God made the angelic clan,
Trails all about the written page,
For in the world's first blossoming age
The light fall of her flying feet
Made Ireland's heart begin to beat,
And still the starry candles flare
To help her light foot here and there,
And still the thoughts of Ireland brood,
Upon her holy quietude.

Nor may I less be counted one
With Davis, Mangan, Ferguson,
Because to him who ponders well
My rhymes more than their rhyming tell
Of the dim wisdoms old and deep,
That God gives unto man in sleep.
For round about my table go
The magical powers to and fro.
In flood and fire and clay and wind,
They huddle from man's pondering mind,
Yet he who treads in austere ways
May surely meet their ancient gaze.
Man ever journeys on with them
After the red rose bordered hem.
Ah, fairies, dancing under the moon,
A druid land, a druid tune!

While still I may I write out true
The love I lived, the dream I knew.
From our birthday until we die,
Is but the winking of an eye.
And we, our singing and our love,
The mariners of night above,
And all the wizard things that go
About my table to and fro,
Are passing on to where may be,
In truth's consuming ecstasy,
No place for love and dream at all,
For God goes by with white foot-fall.
I cast my heart into my rhymes,
That you in the dim coming times
May know how my heart went with them
After the red rose bordered hem.

Yeats's Notes

'To the Rose upon the Rood of Time'

The rose is a favourite symbol with the Irish poets. It has given a name to more than one poem, both Gaelic and English, and is used, not merely in love poems, but in addresses to Ireland, as in De Vere's line, 'The little black rose shall be red at last,' and in Mangan's 'Dark Rosaleen.' I do not, of course, use it in this latter sense.

'The Death of Cuchullin'

Cuchullin (pronounced Cuhoolin) was the great warrior of the Conorian cycle. My poem is founded on a West of Ireland legend given by Curtin in 'Myths and Folk lore of Ireland.' The bardic tale of the death of Cuchullin is very different.

'The White Birds'

The birds of fairyland are white as snow. The 'Danaan shore' is, of course, *Tier-nan-oge*, or fairyland.

'Father Gilligan'

This ballad is founded on the Kerry version of an old folk tale.

'Father O'Hart'

This ballad is founded on the story of a certain 'Father O'Hart,' priest of Coloony in the last century, told by the present priest of Coloony in his most interesting 'History of Ballisodare and Kelvarnet.' The robbery of the lands of Father O'Hart was one of those incidents which occurred some-times, though but rarely, during the time of the penal laws. Catholics, who were forbidden to own landed property, evaded the law by giving some honest Protestant nominal possession of their estates. There are instances on record in which poor men were nominal owners of unnumbered acres.

'The Ballad of the Old Fox Hunter'

This ballad is founded on an incident – probably in turn a transcript from Tipperary tradition – in Kickham's 'Knocknagow.'

'The Lamentation of the Old Pensioner'

This small poem is little more than a translation into verse of the very words of an old Wicklow peasant.

The Wind Among the Reeds

(1899)

The Hosting of the Sidhe

The host is riding from Knocknarea
And over the grave of Clooth-na-bare;
Caolte tossing his burning hair
And Niamh calling *Away, come away:*
Empty your heart of its mortal dream.
The winds awaken, the leaves whirl round,
Our cheeks are pale, our hair is unbound,
Our breasts are heaving, our eyes are a-gleam,
Our arms are waving, our lips are apart;
And if any gaze on our rushing band,
We come between him and the deed of his hand,
We come between him and the hope of his heart.
The host is rushing 'twixt night and day,
And where is there hope or deed as fair?
Caolte tossing his burning hair,
And Niamh calling *Away, come away.*

The Everlasting Voices

O sweet everlasting Voices be still;
Go to the guards of the heavenly fold
And bid them wander obeying your will
Flame under flame, till Time be no more;
Have you not heard that our hearts are old,
That you call in birds, in wind on the hill,
In shaken boughs, in tide on the shore?
O sweet everlasting Voices be still.

The Moods

Time drops in decay,
Like a candle burnt out,
And the mountains and woods
Have their day, have their day;
What one in the rout
Of the fire-born moods,
Has fallen away?

Aedh Tells of the Rose in his Heart

All things uncomely and broken, all things worn out and old,
The cry of a child by the roadway, the creak of a lumbering cart,
The heavy steps of the ploughman, splashing the wintry mould,
Are wronging your image that blossoms a rose in the deeps of my
                                                            heart.

The wrong of unshapely things is a wrong too great to be told;
I hunger to build them anew and sit on a green knoll apart,
With the earth and the sky and the water, remade, like a casket of
                                                            gold
For my dreams of your image that blossoms a rose in the deeps of
                                                       my heart.

The Host of the Air

O'Driscoll drove with a song,
The wild duck and the drake,
From the tall and the tufted reeds
Of the drear Hart Lake.

And he saw how the reeds grew dark
At the coming of night tide,
And dreamed of the long dim hair
Of Bridget his bride.

He heard while he sang and dreamed
A piper piping away,
And never was piping so sad,
And never was piping so gay.

And he saw young men and young girls
Who danced on a level place
And Bridget his bride among them,
With a sad and a gay face.

The dancers crowded about him,
And many a sweet thing said,
And a young man brought him red wine
And a young girl white bread.

But Bridget drew him by the sleeve,
Away from the merry bands,
To old men playing at cards
With a twinkling of ancient hands.

The bread and the wine had a doom,
For these were the hosts of the air;
He sat and played in a dream
Of her long dim hair.

He played with the merry old men
And thought not of evil chance,
Until one bore Bridget his bride
Away from the merry dance.

He bore her away in his arms,
The handsomest young man there,
And his neck and his breast and his arms
Were drowned in her long dim hair.

O'Driscoll scattered the cards
And out of his dream awoke:
Old men and young men and young girls
Were gone like a drifting smoke;

Bnt he heard high up in the air
A piper piping away,
And never was piping so sad,
And never was piping so gay.

Breasal the Fisherman

Although you hide in the ebb and flow
Of the pale tide when the moon has set,
The people of coming days will know
About the casting out of my net,
And how you have leaped times out of mind
Over the little silver cords,
And think that you were hard and unkind,
And blame you with many bitter words.

A Cradle Song

The Danann children laugh, in cradles of wrought gold,
And clap their hands together, and half close their eyes,
For they will ride the North when the ger-eagle flies,
With heavy whitening wings, and a heart fallen cold:
I kiss my wailing child and press it to my breast,
And hear the narrow graves calling my child and me.
Desolate winds that cry over the wandering sea;
Desolate winds that hover in the flaming West;
Desolate winds that beat the doors of Heaven, and beat
The doors of Hell and blow there many a whimpering ghost;
O heart the winds have shaken; the unappeasable host
Is comelier than candles before Maurya's feet.

Into the Twilight

Out-worn heart, in a time out-worn,
Come clear of the nets of wrong and right;
Laugh heart again in the gray twilight,
Sigh, heart, again in the dew of the morn.

Your mother Eire is always young,
Dew ever shining and twilight gray;
Though hope fall from you and love decay,
Burning in fires of a slanderous tongue.

Come, heart, where hill is heaped upon hill:
For there the mystical brotherhood
Of sun and moon and hollow and wood
And river and stream work out their will;

And God stands winding His lonely horn,
And time and the world are ever in flight;
And love is less kind than the gray twilight,
And hope is less dear than the dew of the morn.

The Song of Wandering Aengus

I went out to the hazel wood,
Because a fire was in my head,
And cut and peeled a hazel wand,
And hooked a berry to a thread;
And when white moths were on the wing,
And moth-like stars were flickering out,
I dropped the berry in a stream
And caught a little silver trout.

When I had laid it on the floor
I went to blow the fire a-flame,
But something rustled on the floor,
And someone called me by my name:
It had become a glimmering girl
With apple blossom in her hair
Who called me by my name and ran
And faded through the brightening air.

Though I am old with wandering
Through hollow lands and hilly lands,
I will find out where she has gone,
And kiss her lips and take her hands;
And walk among long dappled grass,
And pluck till time and times are done,
The silver apples of the moon,
The golden apples of the sun.

The Song of the Old Mother

I rise in the dawn, and I kneel and blow
Till the seed of the fire flicker and glow;
And then I must scrub and bake and sweep
Till stars are beginning to blink and peep;
And the young lie long and dream in their bed
Of the matching of ribbons for bosom and head,
And their day goes over in idleness,
And they sigh if the wind but lift a tress:
While I must work because I am old,
And the seed of the fire gets feeble and cold.

The Fiddler of Dooney

When I play on my fiddle in Dooney,
Folk dance like a wave of the sea;
My cousin is priest in Kilvarnet,
My brother in Moharabuiee.

I passed my brother and cousin:
They read in their books of prayer;
I read in my book of songs
I bought at the Sligo fair.

When we come at the end of time,
To Peter sitting in state,
He will smile on the three old spirits,
But call me first through the gate;

For the good are always the merry.
Save by an evil chance,
And the merry love the fiddle
And the merry love to dance:

And when the folk there spy me,
They will all come up to me,
With 'Here is the fiddler of Dooney!'
And dance like a wave of the sea.

The Heart of the Woman

O what to me the little room
That was brimmed up with prayer and rest;
He bade me out into the gloom,
And my breast lies upon his breast.

O what to me my mother's care,
The house where I was safe and warm;
The shadowy blossom of my hair
Will hide us from the bitter storm.

O hiding hair and dewy eyes,
I am no more with life and death,
My heart upon his warm heart lies,
My breath is mixed into his breath.

Aedh Laments the Loss of Love

Pale brows, still hands and dim hair,
I had a beautiful friend
And dreamed that the old despair
Would end in love in the end:
She looked in my heart one day
And saw your image was there;
She has gone weeping away.

Mongan Laments the Change that has Come upon him and his Beloved

Do you not hear me calling, white deer with no horns!
I have been changed to a hound with one red ear;
I have been in the Path of Stones and the Wood of Thorns,
For somebody hid hatred and hope and desire and fear
Under my feet that they follow you night and day.
A man with a hazel wand came without sound;
He changed me suddenly; I was looking another way;
And now my calling is but the calling of a hound;
And Time and Birth and Change are hurrying by.
I would that the boar without bristles had come from the West
And had rooted the sun and moon and stars out of the sky
And lay in the darkness, grunting, and turning to his rest.

Michael Robartes Bids his Beloved Be at Peace

I hear the Shadowy Horses, their long manes a-shake,
Their hoofs heavy with tumult, their eyes glimmering white;
The North unfolds above them clinging, creeping night,
The East her hidden joy before the morning break,
The West weeps in pale dew and sighs passing away,
The South is pouring down roses of crimson fire:
O vanity of Sleep, Hope, Dream, endless Desire,
The Horses of Disaster plunge in the heavy clay:
Beloved, let your eyes half close, and your heart beat
Over my heart, and your hair fall over my breast,
Drowning love's lonely hour in deep twilight of rest,
And hiding their tossing manes and their tumultuous feet.

Hanrahan Reproves the Curlew

O, curlew, cry no more in the air,
Or only to the waters in the West;
Because your crying brings to my mind
Passion-dimmed eyes and long heavy hair
That was shaken out over my breast:
There is enough evil in the crying of wind.

Michael Robartes Remembers Forgotten Beauty

When my arms wrap you round I press
My heart upon the loveliness
That has long faded from the world;
The jewelled crowns that kings have hurled
In shadowy pools, when armies fled;
The love-tales wove with silken thread
By dreaming ladies upon cloth
That has made fat the murderous moth;
The roses that of old time were
Woven by ladies in their hair,
The dew-cold lilies ladies bore
Through many a sacred corridor
Where such gray clouds of incense rose
That only the gods' eyes did not close:
For that pale breast and lingering hand
Come from a more dream-heavy land,
A more dream-heavy hour than this;
And when you sigh from kiss to kiss
I hear white Beauty sighing, too,
For hours when all must fade like dew
But flame on flame, deep under deep.
Throne over throne, where in half sleep
Their swords upon their iron knees
Brood her high lonely mysteries.

A Poet to his Beloved

I bring you with reverent hands
The books of my numberless dreams;
White woman that passion has worn
As the tide wears the dove-gray sands,
And with heart more old than the horn
That is brimmed from the pale fire of time:
White woman with numberless dreams
I bring you my passionate rhyme.

Aedh Gives his Beloved Certain Rhymes

Fasten your hair with a golden pin,
And bind up every wandering tress;
I bade my heart build these poor rhymes:
It worked at them, day out, day in,
Building a sorrowful loveliness
Out of the battles of old times.

You need but lift a pearl-pale hand,
And bind up your long hair and sigh;
And all men's hearts must burn and beat;
And candle-like foam on the dim sand,
And stars climbing the dew-dropping sky,
Live but to light your passing feet.

To My Heart, Bidding it Have No Fear

Be you still, be you still, trembling heart;
Remember the wisdom out of the old days:
Him who trembles before the flame and the flood,
And the winds that blow through the starry ways,
Let the starry winds and the flame and the flood
Cover over and hide, for he has no part
With the proud majestical multitude.

The Cap and Bells

The jester walked in the garden:
The garden had fallen still;
He bade his soul rise upward
And stand on her window-sill.

It rose in a straight blue garment,
When owls began to call:
It had grown wise-tongued by thinking
Of a quiet and light footfall;

But the young queen would not listen;
She rose in her pale night gown;
She drew in the heavy casement
And pushed the latches down.

He bade his heart go to her,
When the owls called out no more;
In a red and quivering garment
It sang to her through the door.

It had grown sweet-tongued by dreaming,
Of a flutter of flower-like hair;
But she took up her fan from the table
And waved it off on the air.

'I have cap and bells' he pondered,
'I will send them to her and die;'
And when the morning whitened
He left them where she went by.

She laid them upon her bosom,
Under a cloud of her hair,
And her red lips sang them a love song:
Till stars grew out of the air.

She opened her door and her window,
And the heart and the soul came through,
To her right hand came the red one,
To her left hand came the blue.

They set up a noise like crickets,
A chattering wise and sweet,
And her hair was a folded flower
And the quiet of love in her feet.

The Valley of the Black Pig

The dews drop slowly and dreams gather: unknown spears
Suddenly hurtle before my dream-awakened eyes,
And then the clash of fallen horsemen and the cries
Of unknown perishing armies beat about my ears.
We who still labour by the cromlec on the shore,
The grey cairn on the hill, when day sinks drowned in dew,
Being weary of the world's empires, bow down to you
Master of the still stars and of the flaming door.

Michael Robartes Asks Forgiveness Because of his Many Moods

If this importunate heart trouble your peace
With words lighter than air,
Or hopes that in mere hoping flicker and cease;
Crumple the rose in your hair;
And cover your lips with odorous twilight and say,
'O Hearts of wind-blown flame!
'O Winds, elder than changing of night and day,
'That murmuring and longing came,
'From marble cities loud with tabors of old
'In dove-gray faery lands;
'From battle banners fold upon purple fold,
'Queens wrought with glimmering hands;
'That saw young Niamh hover with love-lorn face
'Above the wandering tide;
'And lingered in the hidden desolate place,
'Where the last Phoenix died
'And wrapped the flames above his holy head;
'And still murmur and long:
'O Piteous Hearts, changing till change be dead
'In a tumultuous song:'
And cover the pale blossoms of your breast
With your dim heavy hair,
And trouble with a sigh for all things longing for rest
The odorous twilight there.

Aedh Tells of a Valley Full of Lovers

I dreamed that I stood in a valley, and amid sighs,
For happy lovers passed two by two where I stood;
And I dreamed my lost love came stealthily out of the wood
With her cloud-pale eyelids falling on dream-dimmed eyes:
I cried in my dream 'O *women bid the young men lay*
'*Their heads on your knees, and drown their eyes with your hair,*
'*Or remembering hers they will find no other face fair*
'*Till all the valleys of the world have been withered away.*'

Aedh Tells of the Perfect Beauty

O cloud-pale eyelids, dream-dimmed eyes
The poets labouring all their days
To build a perfect beauty in rhyme
Are overthrown by a woman's gaze
And by the unlabouring brood of the skies:
And therefore my heart will bow, when dew
Is dropping sleep, until God burn time,
Before the unlabouring stars and you.

Aedh Hears the Cry of the Sedge

I wander by the edge
Of this desolate lake
Where wind cries in the sedge
Until the axle break
That keeps the stars in their round
And hands hurl in the deep
The banners of East and West
And the girdle of light is unbound,
Your breast will not lie by the breast
Of your beloved in sleep.

Aedh Thinks of Those who have Spoken Evil of his Beloved

Half close your eyelids, loosen your hair,
And dream about the great and their pride;
They have spoken against you everywhere.
But weigh this song with the great and their pride;
I made it out of a mouthful of air,
Their children's children shall say they have lied.

The Blessed

Cumhal called out, bending his head,
Till Dathi came and stood,
With a blink in his eyes at the cave mouth,
Between the wind and the wood.

And Cumhal said, bending his knees,
'I have come by the windy way
'To gather the half of your blessedness
'And learn to pray when you pray.

'I can bring you salmon out of the streams
'And heron out of the skies.'
But Dathi folded his hands and smiled
With the secrets of God in his eyes.

And Cumhal saw like a drifting smoke
All manner of blessed souls,
Women and children, young men with books,
And old men with croziers and stoles.

'Praise God and God's mother,' Dathi said,
'For God and God's mother have sent
'The blessedest souls that walk in the world
'To fill your heart with content.'

'And which is the blessedest,' Cumhal said,
'Where all are comely and good?
'Is it these that with golden thuribles
'Are singing about the wood?'

'My eyes are blinking,' Dathi said,
'With the secrets of God half blind,
'But I can see where the wind goes
'And follow the way of the wind;

'And blessedness goes where the wind goes,
'And when it is gone we are dead;
'I see the blessedest soul in the world
'And he nods a drunken head.

'O blessedness comes in the night and the day
'And whither the wise heart knows;
'And one has seen in the redness of wine
'The Incorruptible Rose,

'That drowsily drops faint leaves on him
'And the sweetness of desire,
'While time and the world are ebbing away
'In twilights of dew and of fire.'

The Secret Rose

Far off, most secret, and inviolate Rose,
Enfold me in my hour of hours; where those
Who sought thee in the Holy Sepulchre,
Or in the wine vat, dwell beyond the stir
And tumult of defeated dreams; and deep
Among pale eyelids, heavy with the sleep
Men have named beauty. Thy great leaves enfold
The ancient beards, the helms of ruby and gold
Of the crowned Magi; and the king whose eyes
Saw the Pierced Hands and Rood of elder rise
In druid vapour and make the torches dim;
Till vain frenzy awoke and he died; and him
Who met Fand walking among flaming dew
By a gray shore where the wind never blew,
And lost the world and Emer for a kiss;
And him who drove the gods out of their liss,
And till a hundred morns had flowered red,
Feasted and wept the barrows of his dead;

And the proud dreaming king who flung the crown
And sorrow away, and calling bard and clown
Dwelt among wine-stained wanderers in deep woods;
And him who sold tillage, and house, and goods,
And sought through lands and islands numberless years,
Until he found with laughter and with tears,
A woman, of so shining loveliness,
That men threshed corn at midnight by a tress,
A little stolen tress. I, too, await
The hour of thy great wind of love and hate.
When shall the stars be blown about the sky,
Like the sparks blown out of a smithy, and die?
Surely thine hour has come, thy great wind blows.
Far off, most secret, and inviolate Rose?

Hanrahan Laments because of his Wanderings

O where is our Mother of Peace
Nodding her purple hood?
For the winds that awakened the stars
Are blowing through my blood.
I would that the death-pale deer
Had come through the mountain side,
And trampled the mountain away,
And drunk up the murmuring tide;
For the winds that awakened the stars
Are blowing through my blood,
And our Mother of Peace has forgot me
Under her purple hood.

The Travail of Passion

When the flaming lute-thronged angelic door is wide;
When an immortal passion breathes in mortal clay;
Our hearts endure the scourge, the plaited thorns, the way
Crowded with bitter faces, the wounds in palm and side,
The hyssop-heavy sponge, the flowers by Kidron stream:
We will bend down and loosen our hair over you,
That it may drop faint perfume, and be heavy with dew,
Lilies of death-pale hope, roses of passionate dream.

The Poet Pleads with his Friend for Old Friends

Though you are in your shining days,
Voices among the crowd
And new friends busy with your praise,
Be not unkind or proud,
But think about old friends the most:
Time's bitter flood will rise,
Your beauty perish and be lost
For all eyes but these eyes.

Hanrahan Speaks to the Lovers of his Songs
in Coming Days

O, colleens, kneeling by your altar rails long hence,
When songs I wove for my beloved hide the prayer,
And smoke from this dead heart drifts through the violet air
And covers away the smoke of myrrh and frankincense;
Bend down and pray for the great sin I wove in song,
Till Maurya of the wounded heart cry a sweet cry,
And call to my beloved and me: 'No longer fly
'Amid the hovering, piteous, penitential throng.'

Aedh Pleads with the Elemental Powers

The Powers whose name and shape no living creature knows
Have pulled the Immortal Rose;
And though the Seven Lights bowed in their dance and wept,
The Polar Dragon slept,
His heavy rings uncoiled from glimmering deep to deep:
When will he wake from sleep?

Great Powers of falling wave and wind and windy fire,
With your harmonious choir
Encircle her I love and sing her into peace,
That my old care may cease;
Unfold your flaming wings and cover out of sight
The nets of day and night.

Dim Powers of drowsy thought, let her no longer be
Like the pale cup of the sea,
When winds have gathered and sun and moon burned dim
Above its cloudy rim;
But let a gentle silence wrought with music flow
Whither her footsteps go.

Aedh Wishes his Beloved were Dead

Were you but lying cold and dead,
And lights were paling out of the West,
You would come hither, and bend your head,
And I would lay my head on your breast;
And you would murmur tender words,
Forgiving me, because you were dead:
Nor would you rise and hasten away,
Though you have the will of the wild birds,
But know your hair was bound and wound
About the stars and moon and sun:
O would beloved that you lay
Under the dock-leaves in the ground,
While lights were paling one by one.

Aedh Wishes for the Cloths of Heaven

Had I the heavens' embroidered cloths,
Enwrought with golden and silver light,
The blue and the dim and the dark cloths
Of night and light and the half light,
I would spread the cloths under your feet:
But I, being poor, have only my dreams;
I have spread my dreams under your feet;
Tread softly because you tread on my dreams.

Mongan Thinks of his Past Greatness

I have drunk ale from the Country of the Young
And weep because I know all things now:
I have been a hazel tree and they hung
The Pilot Star and the Crooked Plough
Among my leaves in times out of mind:
I became a rush that horses tread:
I became a man, a hater of the wind,
Knowing one, out of all things, alone, that his head
Would not lie on the breast or his lips on the hair
Of the woman that he loves, until he dies;
Although the rushes and the fowl of the air
Cry of his love with their pitiful cries.

Yeats's Notes

'The Hosting of the Sidhe'

The powerful and wealthy called the gods of ancient Ireland the Tuatha De Danaan, or the Tribes of the goddess Danu, but the poor called them, and still sometimes call them, the Sidhe, from Aes Sidhe or Sluagh Sidhe, the people of the Faery Hills, as these words are usually explained. Sidhe is also Gaelic for wind, and certainly the Sidhe have much to do with the wind. They journey in whirling winds, the winds that were called the dance of the daughters of Herodias in the Middle Ages, Herodias doubtless taking the place of some old goddess. When the country people see the leaves whirling on the road they bless themselves, because they believe the Sidhe to be passing by. They are almost always said to wear no covering upon their heads, and to let their hair stream out; and the great among them, for they have great and simple, go much upon horseback. If any one becomes too much interested in them, and sees them over much, he loses all interest in ordinary things. I shall write a great deal elsewhere about such enchanted persons, and can give but an example or two now.

A woman near Gort, in Galway, says: 'There is a boy, now, of the Cloran's; but I wouldn't for the world let them think I spoke of him; it's two years since he came from America, and since that time he never went to Mass, or to church, or to fairs, or to market, or to stand on the cross roads, or to hurling, or to nothing. And if any one comes into the house, it's into the room he'll slip, not to see them; and as to work, he has the garden dug to bits, and the whole place smeared with cow dung; and such a crop as was never seen; and the alders all plaited till they look grand. One day he went as far as the chapel; but as soon as he got to the door he turned straight round again, as if he hadn't power to pass it. I wonder he wouldn't get the priest to read a Mass for him, or something; but the crop he has is grand, and you may know well he has some to help him.' One hears many stories of the kind; and a man whose son is believed to go out riding among them at night tells me that he is careless about everything, and lies in bed until it is late in the day. A doctor believes this boy to be mad. Those that are at times 'away,' as it is called, know all things, but are afraid to speak. A countryman at Kiltartan says, 'There was one of the Lydons – John – was away for seven years, lying in his bed, but brought away at nights, and he knew everything; and one, Kearney, up in the mountains, a cousin of his own, lost two hoggets, and came and told him, and he knew the very spot where they were, and told him, and he got them back again. But *they* were vexed at that, and took away the power, so that he never knew anything again, no more than another.' This wisdom is the wisdom of the fools of the Celtic stories, that was above all the wisdom of the wise. Lomna, the fool of Fiann, had so great wisdom that his head, cut from his body, was still able to sing and prophesy; and a writer in the 'Encyclopaedia Britannica' writes that Tristram, in the oldest form of the tale of Tristram and Iseult, drank wisdom, and madness the shadow of wisdom, and not love, out of the magic cup.

The great of the old times are among the Tribes of Danu, and are kings and queens among them. Caolte was a companion of Fiann; and years after his death he appeared to a king in a forest, and was a flaming man, that he might lead him in the darkness. When the king asked him who he was, he said, 'I am your candlestick.' I do not remember where I have read this story, and I have, maybe, half forgotten it. Niam was a beautiful woman of the Tribes of Danu, that led Oïsin to the Country of the Young, as their country is called; I have written about her in 'The Wandering of Usheen;' and he came back, at last, to bitterness and weariness.

Knocknarea is in Sligo, and the country people say that Maeve, still a great queen of the western Sidhe, is buried in the cairn of stones upon it. I have written of Clooth-na-Bare in 'The Celtic Twilight.' She 'went all over the world, seeking a lake deep enough to drown her faery life, of which she had grown weary, leaping from hill to hill, and setting up a cairn of stones wherever her feet lighted, until, at last, she found the deepest water in the world in little Lough Ia, on the top of the bird mountain, in Sligo.' I forget, now, where I heard this story, but it may have been from a priest at Collooney. Clooth-na-Bare would mean the old woman of Bare, but is evidently a corruption of Cailleac Bare, the old woman Bare, who, under the names Bare, and Berah, and Beri, and Verah, and Dera, and Dhira, appears in the legends of many places. Mr O'Grady found her haunting Lough Liath high up on the top of a mountain of the Fews, the Slieve Fuadh, or Slieve G-Cullain of old times, under the name of the Cailleac Buillia. He describes Lough Liath as a desolate moon-shaped lake, with made wells and sunken passages upon its borders, and beset by marsh and heather and gray boulders, and closes his 'Flight of the Eagle' with a long rhapsody upon mountain and lake, because of the heroic tales and beautiful old myths that have hung about them always. He identifies the Cailleac Buillia with that Meluchra who persuaded Fionn to go to her amid the waters of Lough Liath, and so changed him with her enchantments, that, though she had to free him because of the threats of the Fiana, his hair was ever afterwards as white as snow. To this day the Tribes of the Goddess Danu that are in the waters beckon to men, and drown them in the waters; and Bare, or Dhira, or Meluchra, or whatever name one likes the best, is, doubt less, the name of a mistress among them. Meluchra was daughter of Cullain; and Cullain Mr O'Grady calls, upon I know not what authority, a form of Lir, the master of waters. The people of the waters have been in all ages beautiful and changeable and lascivious, or beautiful and wise and lonely, for water is everywhere the signature of the fruitfulness of the body and of the fruitfulness of dreams. The white hair of Fionn may be but another of the troubles of those that come to unearthly wisdom and earthly trouble, and the threats and violence of the Fiana against her, a different form of the threats and violence the country people use, to make the Tribes of Danu give up those that are 'away.' Bare is now often called an ugly old woman; but Dr Joyce says that one of her old names was Aebhin, which means beautiful. Aebhen was the goddess of the tribes of northern Leinster; and the lover she had made immortal, and who loved her perfectly, left her, and put on mortality, to fight among them against the stranger, and died on the strand of Clontarf.

Aedh, Hanrahan and Michael Robartes in these poems
These are personages in 'The Secret Rose;' but, with the exception of some of Hanrahan's and one of Aedh's poems, the poems are not out of that book. I have used them in this book more as principles of the mind than as actual personages. It is probable that only students of the magical tradition will understand me when I say that 'Michael Robartes' is fire reflected in water, and that Hanrahan is fire blown by the wind, and that Aedh, whose name is not merely the Irish form of Hugh, but the Irish for fire, is fire burning, by itself. To put it in a different way, Hanrahan is the simplicity of an imagination too changeable to gather permanent possessions, or the adoration of the shepherds; and Michael Robartes is the pride of the imagination brooding upon the greatness of its possessions, or the adoration of the Magi; while Aedh is the myrrh and frankincense that the imagination offers continually before all that it loves.

'Aedh Pleads with the Elemental Powers', 'Mongan Thinks of his Past Greatness', 'Aedh Hears the Cry of the Sedge'
The Rose has been for many centuries a symbol of spiritual love and supreme beauty. The Count Goblet D'Alviella thinks that it was once a symbol of the sun, – itself a principal symbol of the divine nature, and the symbolic heart of things. The lotus was in some Eastern countries imagined blossoming upon the Tree of Life, as the Flower of Life, and is thus represented in Assyrian bas-reliefs. Because the Rose, the flower sacred to the Virgin Mary, and the flower that Apuleius' adventurer ate, when he was changed out of the ass's shape and received into the fellowship of Isis, is the western Flower of Life, I have imagined it growing upon the Tree of Life. I once stood beside a man in Ireland when he saw it growing there in a vision, that seemed to have rapt him out of his body. He saw the garden of Eden walled about, and on the top of a high mountain, as in certain mediaeval diagrams,

and after passing the Tree of Knowledge, on which grew fruit full of trou-
bled faces, and through whose branches flowed, he was told, sap that was
human souls, he came to a tall, dark tree, with little bitter fruits, and was
shown a kind of stair or ladder going up through the tree, and told to go
up; and near the top of the tree, a beautiful woman, like the Goddess of Life
associated with the tree in Assyria, gave him a rose that seemed to have been
growing upon the tree. One finds the Rose in the Irish poets, sometimes as
a religious symbol, as in the phrase, 'the Rose of Friday,' meaning the Rose
of austerity, in a Gaelic poem in Dr Hyde's 'Religious Songs of Connacht;'
and, I think, as a symbol of woman's beauty in the Gaelic song, 'Roseen
Dubh;' and a symbol of Ireland in Mangan's adaptation of 'Roseen Dubh,'
'My Dark Rosaleen,' and in Mr Aubrey de Vere's 'The Little Black Rose.'
I do not know any evidence to prove whether this symbol came to Ireland
with mediaeval Christianity, or whether it has come down from Celtic
times. I have read somewhere that a stone engraved with a Celtic god, who
holds what looks like a rose in one hand, has been found somewhere in
England; but I cannot find the reference, though I certainly made a note of
it. If the Rose was really a symbol of Ireland among the Gaelic poets, and
if 'Roseen Dubh' is really a political poem, as some think, one may feel
pretty certain that the ancient Celts associated the Rose with Eire, or Fotla,
or Banba – goddesses who gave their names to Ireland – or with some prin-
cipal god or goddess, for such symbols are not suddenly adopted or invented,
but come out of mythology.

I have made the Seven Lights, the constellation of the Bear, lament for
the theft of the Rose, and I have made the Dragon, the constellation Draco,
the guardian of the Rose, because these constellations move about the pole
of the heavens, the ancient Tree of Life in many countries, and are often
associated with the Tree of Life in mythology. It is this Tree of Life that I
have put into the 'Song of Mongan' under its common Irish form of a hazel;
and, because it had sometimes the stars for fruit, I have hung upon it 'the
Crooked Plough' and the 'Pilot' star, as Gaelic-speaking Irishmen sometimes
call the Bear and the North star. I have made it an axle-tree in 'Aedh hears
the Cry of the Sedge', for this was another ancient way of representing it.

'The Host of the Air'

Some writers distinguish between the Sluagh Gaoith, the host of the air, and
Sluagh Sidhe, the host of the Sidhe, and describe the host of the air as of a
peculiar malignancy. Dr Joyce says, 'of all the different kinds of goblins …
air demons were most dreaded by the people. They lived among clouds,
and mists, and rocks, and hated the human race with the utmost malignity.'
A very old Arann charm, which contains the words 'Send God, by his
strength,between us and the host of the Sidhe, between us and the host of

the air,' seems also to distinguish among them. I am inclined, however, to think that the distinction came in with Christianity and its belief about the prince of the air, for the host of the Sidhe, as I have already explained, are closely associated with the wind.

They are said to steal brides just after their marriage, and sometimes in a blast of wind. A man in Galway says, 'At Aughanish there were two couples came to the shore to be married, and one of the newly married women was in the boat with the priest, and they going back to the island; and a sudden blast of wind came, and the priest said some blessed words that were able to save himself, but the girl was swept.'

This woman was drowned; but more often the persons who are taken 'get the touch,' as it is called, and fall into a half dream, and grow indifferent to all things, for their true life has gone out of the world, and is among the hills and the forts of the Sidhe. A faery doctor has told me that his wife 'got the touch' at her marriage because there was one of them wanted her; and the way he knew for certain was, that when he took a pitchfork out of the rafters, and told her it was a broom, she said, 'It is a broom.' She was, the truth is, in the magical sleep, to which people have given a new name lately, that makes the imagination so passive that it can be moulded by any voice in any world into any shape. A mere likeness of some old woman, or even old animal, some one or some thing the Sidhe have no longer a use for, is believed to be left instead of the person who is 'away;' this some one or some thing can, it is thought, be driven away by threats, or by violence (though I have heard country women say that violence is wrong), which perhaps awakes the soul out of the magical sleep. The story in the poem is founded on an old Gaelic ballad that was sung and translated for me by a woman at Ballisodare in County Sligo; but in the ballad the husband found the keeners keening his wife when he got to his house. She was 'swept' at once; but the Sidhe are said to value those the most whom they but cast into a half dream, which may last for years, for they need the help of a living person in most of the things they do. There are many stories of people who seem to die and be buried – though the country people will tell you it is but some one or some thing put in their place that dies and is buried – and yet are brought back afterwards. These tales are perhaps memories of true awakenings out of the magical sleep, moulded by the imagination, under the influence of a mystical doctrine which it understands too literally, into the shape of some well-known traditional tale. One does not hear them as one hears the others, from the persons who are 'away,' or from their wives or husbands; and one old man, who had often seen the Sidhe, began one of them with 'Maybe it is all vanity.'

Here is a tale that a friend of mine heard in the Burren hills, and it is a type of all: –

'There was a girl to be married, and she didn't like the man, and she cried when the day was coming, and said she wouldn't go along with him. And the mother said, 'Get into the bed, then, and I'll say that you're sick.' And so she did. And when the man came the mother said to him, 'You can't get her, she's sick in the bed.' And he looked in and said, 'That's not my wife that's in the bed, it's some old hag.' And the mother began to cry and to roar. And he went out and got two hampers of turf, and made a fire, that they thought he was going to burn the house down. And when the fire was kindled, 'Come out now,' says he, 'and we'll see who you are, when I'll put you on the fire.' And when she heard that, she gave one leap, and was out of the house, and they saw, then, it was an old hag she was. Well, the man asked the advice of an old woman, and she bid him go to a faery-bush that was near, and he might get some word of her. So he went there at night, and saw all sorts of grand people, and they in carriages or riding on horses, and among them he could see the girl he came to look for. So he went again to the old woman, and she said, 'If you can get the three bits of blackthorn out of her hair, you'll get her again.' So that night he went again, and that time he only got hold of a bit of her hair. But the old woman told him that was no use, and that he was put back now, and it might be twelve nights before he'd get her. But on the fourth night he got the third bit of black-thorn, and he took her, and she came away with him. He never told the mother he had got her; but one day she saw her at a fair, and, says she, 'That's my daughter; I know her by the smile and by the laugh of her,' and she with a shawl about her head. So the husband said, 'You're right there, and hard I worked to get her.' She spoke often of the grand things she saw under-ground, and how she used to have wine to drink, and to drive out in a carriage with four horses every night. And she used to be able to see her husband when he came to look for her, and she was greatly afraid he'd get a drop of the wine, for then he would have come underground and never left it again. And she was glad herself to come to earth again, and not to be left there.'

The old Gaelic literature is full of the appeals of the Tribes of the goddess Danu to mortals whom they would bring into their country; but the song of Midher to the beautiful Etain, the wife of the king who was called Echaid the ploughman, is the type of all.

'O beautiful woman, come with me to the marvellous land where one listens to a sweet music, where one has spring flowers in one's hair, where the body is like snow from head to foot, where no one is sad or silent, where teeth are white and eyebrows are black ... cheeks red like foxglove in flower ... Ireland is beautiful, but not so beautiful as the Great Plain I call you to. The beer of Ireland is heady, but the beer of the Great Plain is much more heady. How marvellous is the country I am speaking of! Youth does not grow old there. Streams with warm flood flow there; sometimes mead, sometimes wine. Men are charming and without a blot there, and love is not forbidden there. O woman, when you come into my powerful country you will wear a crown of gold upon your head. I will give you the flesh of swine, and you will have beer and milk to drink, O beautiful woman. O beautiful woman, come with me!'

'A Cradle Song', 'Michael Robartes Asks Forgiveness because of his Many Moods'
I use the wind as a symbol of vague desires and hopes, not merely because the Sidhe are in the wind, or because the wind bloweth as it listeth, but because wind and spirit and vague desire have been associated everywhere. A highland scholar tells me that his country people use the wind in their talk and in their proverbs as I use it in my poem.

'The Song of Wandering Aengus'
The Tribes of the goddess Danu can take all shapes, and those that are in the waters take often the shape of fish. A woman of Burren, in Galway, says, 'There are more of them in the sea than on the land, and they sometimes try to come over the side of the boat in the form of fishes, for they can take their choice shape.' At other times they are beautiful women; and another Galway woman says, 'Surely those things are in the sea as well as on land. My father was out fishing one night off Tyrone. And something came beside the boat that had eyes shining like candles. And then a wave came in, and a storm rose all in a minute, and whatever was in the wave, the weight of it had like to sink the boat. And then they saw that it was a woman in the sea that had the shining eyes. So my father went to the priest, and he bid him always to take a drop of holy water and a pinch of salt out in the boat with him, and nothing could harm him.'

The poem was suggested to me by a Greek folk song; but the folk belief of Greece is very like that of Ireland, and I certainly thought, when I wrote it, of Ireland, and of the spirits that are in Ireland. An old man who was cutting a quickset hedge near Gort, in Galway, said, only the other day, 'One time I was cutting timber over in Inchy, and about eight o'clock one morning, when I got there, I saw a girl picking nuts, with her hair hanging down over her shoulders; brown hair; and she had a good, clean face, and she was tall, and nothing on her head, and her dress no way gaudy, but simple. And when she felt me coming she gathered herself up, and was gone, as if the earth had swallowed her up. And I followed her, and looked for her, but I never could see her again from that day to this, never again.'

The county Galway people use the word 'clean' in its old sense of fresh and comely.

'Michael Robartes Bids his Beloved Be at Peace'

November, the old beginning of winter, or of the victory of the Fomor, or powers of death, and dismay, and cold, and darkness, is associated by the Irish people with the horse-shaped Púcas, who are now mischievous spirits, but were once Fomorian divinities. I think that they may have some connection with the horses of Mannannan, who reigned over the country of the dead, where the Fomorian Tethra reigned also; and the horses of Mannannan, though they could cross the land as easily as the sea, are constantly associated with the waves. Some neo-platonist, I forget who, describes the sea as a symbol of the drifting indefinite bitterness of life, and I believe there is like symbolism intended in the many Irish voyages to the islands of enchantment, or that there was, at any rate, in the mythology out of which these stories have been shaped. I follow much Irish and other mythology, and the magical tradition, in associating the North with night and sleep, and the East, the place of sunrise, with hope, and the South, the place of the sun when at its height, with passion and desire, and the West, the place of sunset, with fading and dreaming things.

'Mongan Laments the Change that has Come upon him and his Beloved',
'Hanrahan Laments because of his Wanderings'

My deer and hound are properly related to the deer and hound that flicker in and out of the various tellings of the Arthurian legends, leading different knights upon adventures, and to the hounds and to the hornless deer at the beginning of, I think, all tellings of Oisin's journey to the country of the young. The hound is certainly related to the Hounds of Annwvyn or of Hades, who are white, and have red ears, and were heard, and are, perhaps, still heard by Welsh peasants following some flying thing in the night winds; and is probably related to the hounds that Irish country people believe will awake and seize the souls of the dead if you lament them too loudly or too soon, and to the hound the son of Setanta killed, on what was certainly, in the first form of the tale, a visit to the Celtic Hades. An old woman told a friend and myself that she saw what she thought were white birds, flying over an enchanted place, but found, when she got near, that they had dog's heads; and I do not doubt that my hound and these dog-headed birds are of the same family. I got my hound and deer out of a last century Gaelic poem about Oisin's journey to the country of the young. After the hunting of the hornless deer, that leads him to the seashore, and while he is riding over the sea with Niam, he sees amid the waters – I have not the Gaelic poem by me, and describe it from memory – a young man following a girl who has a golden apple, and afterwards a hound with one red ear following a deer with no horns. This hound and this deer seem plain images of the desire of man 'which is for the woman,' and 'the desire of the woman which is for the desire of the man,' and of all desires that are as these. I have read them in this way in 'The Wanderings of Usheen' or Oisin, and have made my lover sigh because he has seen in their faces 'the immortal desire of immortals.' A solar mythologist would perhaps say that the girl with the golden apple was once the winter, or night, carrying the sun away, and the deer without horns, like the boar without bristles, darkness flying the light. He would certainly, I think, say that when Cuchullain, whom Professor Rhys calls a solar hero, hunted the enchanted deer of Slieve Fuadh, because the battle fury was still on him, he was the sun pursuing clouds, or cold, or darkness. I have understood them in this sense in 'Hanrahan laments because of his wandering,' and made Hanrahan long for the day when they, fragments of ancestral darkness, will overthrow the world. The desire of the woman, the flying darkness, it is all one! The image – a cross, a man preaching in the wilderness, a dancing Salome, a lily in a girl's hand, a flame leaping, a globe with wings, a pale sunset over still waters – is an eternal act; but our understandings are temporal and understand but a little at a time.

The man in my poem who has a hazel wand may have been Aengus, Master of Love; and I have made the boar without bristles come out of the West, because the place of sunset was in Ireland, as in other countries, a place of symbolic darkness and death.

'The Cap and Bells'

I dreamed this story exactly as I have written it, and dreamed another long dream after it, trying to make out its meaning, and whether I was to write it in prose or verse. The first dream was more a vision than a dream, for it was beautiful and coherent, and gave me the sense of illumination and exaltation that one gets from visions, while the second dream was confused and meaningless. The poem has always meant a great deal to me, though, as is the way with symbolic poems, it has not always meant quite the same thing. Blake would have said 'the authors are in eternity,' and I am quite sure they can only be questioned in dreams.

'The Valley of the Black Pig'

All over Ireland there are prophecies of the coming rout of the enemies of Ireland, in a certain Valley of the Black Pig, and these prophecies are, no doubt, now, as they were in the Fenian days, a political force. I have heard of one man who would not give any money to the Land League, because the Battle could not be until the close of the century; but, as a rule, periods of trouble bring prophecies of its near coming. A few years before my time, an old man who lived at Lisadell, in Sligo, used to fall down in a fit and rave out descriptions of the Battle; and a man in Sligo has told me that it will be so great a battle that the horses shall go up to their fetlocks in blood, and that their girths, when it is over, will rot from their bellies for lack of a hand to unbuckle them. The battle is a mythological battle, and the black pig is one with the bristleless boar, that killed Dearmod, in November, upon the western end of Ben Bulben; Misroide MacDatha's sow, whose carving brought on so great a battle; 'the croppy black sow,' and 'the cutty black sow' of Welsh November rhymes ('Celtic Heathendom,' pages 509–516); the boar that killed Adonis; the boar that killed Attis; and the pig embodiment of Typhon ('Golden Bough,' II. pages 26, 31). The pig seems to have been originally a genius of the corn, and, seemingly because the too great power of their divinity makes divine things dangerous to mortals, its flesh was forbidden to many eastern nations; but as the meaning of the prohibition was forgotten, abhorrence took the place of reverence, pigs and boars grew into types of evil, and were described as the enemies of the very gods they once typified ('Golden Bough,' II. 26–31, 56–57). The Pig would, therefore, become the Black Pig, a type of cold and of winter that awake in November, the old beginning of winter, to do battle with the summer, and with the fruit and leaves, and finally, as I suggest; and as I believe, for the purposes of poetry; of the darkness that will at last destroy the gods and the world. The country people say there is no shape for a spirit to take so dangerous as the shape of a pig; and a Galway blacksmith – and blacksmiths are thought to be especially protected – says he would be afraid to meet a pig on the road at night; and another Galway man tells this story: 'There was a man coming the road from Gort to Garryland one night and he had a drop taken; and before him, on the road, he saw a pig walking; and having a drop in, he gave a shout, and made a kick at it, and bid it get out of that. And by the time he got home, his arm was swelled from the shoulder to be as big as a bag, and he couldn't use his hand with the pain of it. And his wife brought him, after a few days, to a woman that used to do cures at Rahasane. And on the road all she could do would hardly keep him from lying down to sleep on the grass. And when they got to the woman she knew all that happened; and, says she, it's well for you that your wife didn't let you fall asleep on the grass, for if you had done that but even for one instant, you'd be a lost man.'

It is possible that bristles were associated with fertility, as the tail certainly was, for a pig's tail is stuck into the ground in Courland, that the corn may grow abundantly, and the tails of pigs, and other animal embodiments of the corn genius, are dragged over the ground to make it fertile in different countries. Professor Rhys, who considers the bristleless boar a symbol of darkness and cold, rather than of winter and cold, thinks it was without bristles because the darkness is shorn away by the sun. It may have had different meanings, just as the scourging of the man-god has had different though not contradictory meanings in different epochs of the world.

The Battle should, I believe, be compared with three other battles; a battle the Sidhe are said to fight when a person is being taken away by them; a battle they are said to fight in November for the harvest; the great battle the Tribes of the goddess Danu fought, according to the Gaelic chroniclers, with the Fomor at Moy Tura, or the Towery Plain.

I have heard of the battle over the dying both in County Galway and in the Isles of Arann, an old Arann fisherman having told me that it was fought over two of his children, and that he found blood in a box he had for keeping fish, when it was over; and I have written about it, and given examples elsewhere. A faery doctor, on the borders of Galway and Clare, explained it as a battle between the friends and enemies of the dying, the one party trying to take them, the other trying to save them from being taken. It may once, when the land of the Sidhe was the only other world, and when every man who died was carried thither, have always accompanied death. I suggest that the battle between the Tribes of the goddess Danu, the powers of light, and warmth, and fruitfulness, and goodness, and the Fomor, the powers of darkness, and cold, and barrenness, and badness upon the Towery Plain, was the establishment of the habitable world, the rout of the ancestral darkness; that the battle among the Sidhe for the harvest is the annual battle of summer and winter; that the battle among the Sidhe at a man's death is the battle of life and death; and that the battle of the Black Pig is the battle between the manifest world and the ancestral darkness at the end of all things; and that all these battles are one, the battle of all things with shadowy decay. Once a symbolism has possessed the imagination of large numbers of men, it becomes, as I believe, an embodiment of disembodied powers, and repeats itself in dreams and visions, age after age.

'The Secret Rose'

I find that I have unintentionally changed the old story of Conchobar's death. He did not see the crucifixion in a vision, but was told about it. He had been struck by a ball, made of the dried brain of a dead enemy, and hurled out of a sling; and this ball had been left in his head, and his head had been mended, the Book of Leinster says, with thread of gold because his hair was like gold. Keating, a writer of the time of Elizabeth, says, 'In that state did he remain seven years, until the Friday on which Christ was crucified, according to some historians; and when he saw the unusual changes of the creation and the eclipse of the sun and the moon at its full, he asked of Bucrach, a Leinster Druid, who was along with him, what was it that brought that unusual change upon the planets of Heaven and Earth. 'Jesus Christ, the son of God,' said the Druid, 'who is now being crucified by the Jews.' 'That is a pity,' said Conchobar; 'were I in his presence I would kill those who were putting him to death.' And with that he brought out his sword, and rushed at a woody grove which was convenient to him, and began to cut and fell it; and what he said was, that if he were among the Jews that was the usage he would give them, and from the excessiveness of his fury which seized upon him, the ball started out of his head, and some of the brain came after it, and in that way he died. The wood of Lanshraigh, in Feara Rois, is the name by which that shrubby wood is called.'

I have imagined Cuchullain meeting Fand 'walking among flaming dew.' The story of their love is one of the most beautiful of our old tales. Two birds, bound one to another with a chain of gold, came to a lake side where Cuchullain and the host of Uladh was encamped, and sang so sweetly that all the host fell into a magic sleep. Presently they took the shape of two beautiful women, and cast a magical weakness upon Cuchullain, in which he lay for a year. At the year's end an Aengus, who was probably Aengus the master of love, one of the greatest of the children of the goddess Danu, came and sat upon his bedside, and sang how Fand, the wife of Mannannan, the master of the sea, and of the islands of the dead, loved him; and that if he would come into the country of the gods, where there was wine and gold and silver, Fand, and Laban her sister, would heal him of his magical weakness. Cuchullain went to the country of the gods, and, after being for a month the lover of Fand, made her a promise to meet her at a place called 'the Yew at the Strand's End,' and came back to the earth. Emer, his mortal wife, won his love again, and Mannannan came to 'the Yew at the Strand's End,' and carried Fand away. When Cuchullain saw her going, his love for her fell upon him again, and he went mad, and wandered among the mountains without food or drink, until he was at last cured by a Druid drink of forgetfulness.

I have founded the man 'who drove the gods out of their Liss,' or fort, upon something I have read about Caolte after the battle of Gabra, when almost all his companions were killed, driving the gods out of their Liss, either at Osraighe, now Ossory, or at Eas Ruaidh, now Asseroe, a waterfall at Ballyshannon, where Ilbreac, one of the children of the goddess Danu, had a Liss. I am writing away from most of my books, and have not been able to find the passage; but I certainly read it somewhere.

I have founded 'the proud dreaming king' upon Fergus, the son of Roigh, the legendary poet of 'the quest of the bull of Cualge,' as he is in the ancient story of Deirdre, and in modern poems by Ferguson. He married Nessa, and Ferguson makes him tell how she took him 'captive in a single look.'

> 'I am but an empty shade,
> Far from life and passion laid;
> Yet does sweet remembrance thrill
> All my shadowy being still.'

Presently, because of his great love, he gave up his throne to Conchobar, her son by another, and lived out his days feasting, and fighting, and hunting. His promise never to refuse a feast from a certain comrade, and the mischief that came by his promise, and the vengeance he took afterwards, are a principal theme of the poets. I have explained my imagination of him in 'Fergus and the Druid,' and in a little song in the second act of 'The Countess Kathleen.'

I have founded him 'who sold tillage, and house, and goods,' upon something in 'The Red Pony,' a folk tale in Mr Larminie's 'West Irish Folk Tales.' A young man 'saw a light before him on the high road. When he came as far, there was an open box on the road, and a light coming up out of it. He took up the box. There was a lock of hair in it. Presently he had to go to become the servant of a king for his living. There were eleven boys. When they were going out into the stable at ten o'clock, each of them took a light but he. He took no candle at all with him. Each of them went into his own stable. When he went into his stable he opened the box. He left it in a hole in the wall. The light was great. It was twice as much as in the other stables.' The king hears of it, and makes him show him the box. The king says, 'You must go and bring me the woman to whom the hair belongs.' In the end, the young man, and not the king, marries the woman.

NOTES AND INDEXES

Notes on the Poems

The Wanderings of Oisin and Other Poems (1889)

p. 3   'The Wanderings of Oisin'

Yeats's choice of subject-matter is significant in terms of Celticism and Irish cultural nationalism. Oisin is the same as 'Ossian', the legendary author of the supposed Gaelic originals of the Scottish Ossianic poems of James Macpherson (1736–96), which had enjoyed popularity and esteem not just in the British Isles but in Europe and America. These had come to stand for a quintessentially Celtic or Gaelic sensibility. Oisin is a warrior–bard, son of Finn mac Cumhail ('Finn McCool': modern Irish 'Fionn mac Cumhail'), who himself was the leader of a band of warriors called the Fianna (or Fenians).

Subtitle: 'And How a Demon Trapped Him'. The idea of the 'Demon' or the demonic was of abiding interest to Yeats. His adopted name in the Hermetic Order of the Golden Dawn was *Demon Est Deus Inversus* – 'a demon is (a) god inverted'. In both versions of his great occult synthesis, *A Vision* (1925) and (1937), the concept of the 'Daemon' is important. In the 1925 version this is spelt 'Daimon' and is undoubtedly feminine. Yeats is conscious of the word's original sense of 'spirit', often translated by the Latin 'genius'. But he is equally conscious of the latter-day connotations of malignity. Niam is the Demon in 'The Wanderings of Oisin'. She is one of the 'Sidhe', the people of the wind, the fairies, or perhaps more properly 'people of Faery': they are not usually diminutive in ancient Irish tradition, and are perhaps reminiscent of the Germanic elves. They are immortal and alien, and while a beautiful woman of Faery may entice away a mortal man, as in the Scottish ballad of 'Thomas the Rhymer', it is often the case that, as in that ballad, no lasting happiness ensues. Indeed, it is possible that the Sidhe bear ill will towards humanity. In 'The Hosting of the Sidhe', from *The Wind Among the Reeds*, Niam (there spelt 'Niamh') joins in the chorus of '*if any gaze on our rushing band, / We come between him and the deed of his hand, / We come between him and the hope of his heart*'.

Part I

Patrick. St Patrick (*c*.385–*c*.461) is traditionally supposed to have introduced Christianity to Ireland from Britain.

p. 3, 'Bran, Sgeolan, and Lomair'. The hounds of Finn.

'Lough Laen'. Lake in Leinster, with which its name is associated (Laighin [Irish]: 'Leinster').

'Gavra'. Or Gabhra, a plain in Leinster where the Fianna were defeated in battle.

'Oscar'. Finn's son, killed at the battle of Gabhra.

p. 4, 'Eman'. Emain Macha (near Armagh), in ancient Irish tradition the dwelling place of the Kings of Ulster.

p. 5, 'Fin'. i.e., Finn.

'King / Of the Young.' Because they were immortal, the Sidhe might be referred to as 'the Young'. For instance, their home beyond the western ocean was called Tír na nÓg: 'The Land of the Young'.

Part II

p. 18, 'Danaan'. Pertaining to the Tuatha Dé Danann, 'The People of the Goddess Danu', another name for the Sidhe.

p. 19, 'Eri'. For Irish Éire: 'Ireland'.

p. 21, 'Mananan'. Manannán mac Lir, presumed to have been the god of the sea in pagan Ireland.

p. 25, 'Conan'. Another of the Fenians.

Part III

p. 28, 'bell-branch'. A magical branch which induces sleep when shaken.

'Sennachies'. Story-tellers: Irish *seanchaí*.

p. 29, 'Conor'. King of Ulster in the days of Cuchulain (see following note). Usually spelt 'Conchubar', and spelt thus by Yeats in later works.

'Blanid'. Legendary heroine. Carried away as a spoil of battle, she killed her taker and was herself killed in revenge. 'Mac Nessa': Conchubar (or Conor) mac Nessa, King of Ulster in heroic times. 'Cuchulin'. Cuchulain, or Cú Chulain, champion warrior of Ulster in the days of King Conchubar, and hero of the epic saga *Táin Bó Cuailgne*, 'The Cattle Raid of Cooley'. See note to 'The Death of Cuchullin' (below). 'Fergus' was King of Ulster, but his wife Nessa persuaded him to abdicate in favour of her son, and his stepson, Conchubar.

'Barach'. Enticed Fergus away from Deirdre and the sons of Usna so that the latter could be killed on Conchubar's orders, since they were protecting Deirdre and Conchubar coveted her for himself.

'Balor'. A leader of the Fomorians, the hosts of darkness.

'Grania'. Irish Gráinne, heroine of the tale of 'Diarmuid and Gráinne'.

p. 30, 'Meridian isle'. Legendary island on the equator.

p. 32, 'rath'. Irish for a fort or fortified homestead.

p. 33, 'Crevroe or on broad Knockfefin'. There is no certain identification, though Crevroe sounds like an anglicisation of *Craobh ruadh*, 'Red Branch', the emblem of the ancient dynasty of Ulster resident at Emain Macha near Armagh.

p. 34, 'Caolte'. One of the Fenians, often spelt 'Caoilte'.

p. 36   'Time and the Witch Vivien'

Vivien is the enchantress (sometimes called Nimue) who in Arthurian legend stole the heart of Merlin but then imprisoned him in an oak, reputedly located in Carmarthen.

p. 39   'The Stolen Child'

Alludes to the notion, once quite common among the Irish peasantry, that the fairies might steal young children.

'Slewth Wood'. Or Sleuth Wood. It is on the southern shores of Lough Gill, south-east of Sligo, and more commonly known as Slish Wood.

'Rosses'. Rosses Point, a seaside village north-west of Sligo, or the headland on which it sits.

'Glen-Car'. Glencar is a valley containing a lough and a waterfall north-east of Sligo.

p. 40   'Girl's Song'

This poem made its way into Yeats's short story 'Dhoya', from *John Sherman and Dhoya* (1891). It is not, of course, to be confused with 'Girl's Song' from Yeats's *Words for Music Perhaps*, which is to be found in *The Winding Stair and Other Poems* (1933).

p. 41   'Ephemera'

Yeats removed the last ten lines in subsequent editions.

p. 43   'Kanva, the Indian, on God'

Kanva is a sage in the Sanskrit play *Śakuntalā*. The pantheism of this poem suggests that Yeats might have thought that Indian philosophy was akin to that of Druidism, which was also thought to be pantheistic.

p. 45   'Jealousy'

In subsequent collections becomes 'Anashuya and Vijaya'.

Anashuya. In Hindu mythology, Anashuya is a daughter of the creator and sage Daksha.

Vijaya. The name means 'victorious'.

p. 45, Amrita. In Hindu mythology, the drink of the gods and the elixir of immortality.

Brahma. Brahmā is the Hindu god of creation, and is often said to be a son of Brahman, the supreme being, with whom he is not to be confused.

p. 46, Kama. As Yeats explains, 'the Indian Cupid', or the Indian god of love.

p. 47, 'Golden Peak'. Hemakūta, a sacred mountain said to lie north of the Himalayas.

p. 48   'Song of the Last Arcadian'

Best known by its title in subsequent collections, 'The Song of the Happy Shepherd'.

'Arcady'. Arcadia, an idealised, mountainous region of southern Greece, imagined in the pastoral tradition as the home of peaceful and carefree shepherds.

'Chronos'. The Greek word for time, here personified. The personification became confused with Kronos, the name of one of the Titans, called Saturn by the Romans.

'rood'. Slightly archaic word for the cross on which Christ was crucified.

'Attic'. Of or pertaining to Attica, the region of Greece of which Athens was the chief city.

p. 50   'King Goll'

In a note of 1887, Yeats explains that Goll became mad after a battle. The version of the story he was using seems to have been influenced by the legend of *Suibhne Geilt* ('Mad Sweeney'), known from the twelfth-century manuscript *Buile Shuibhne* ('The Frenzy of Sweeney'), which has been translated as *Sweeney Astray* (1984) by Seamus Heaney.

'Eman'. Emain Macha, seat of the kings of Ulster in the heroic age.

'Morna'. Yeats appears to be associating Goll with the family of Goll mac Morna, one of the followers of Finn mac Cumhail, though this is a very uncertain association.

p. 52, 'ulalu'. A cry of mourning.

p. 52   'The Meditation of the Old Fisherman'

'creel'. A wicker basket.

p. 53   'The Ballad of Moll Magee'

'Kinsale'. Seaport in Co. Cork.

p. 58   'Mosada'

First published in *The Dublin University Review* (1886).

Scene I

p. 58, stage direction, 'Azubia'. The identification is uncertain, but this may be the village of Zubia in Granada.

p. 59, 'Azolar'. Appears to be a fictional character.

'Alpujarras'. Mountains in Andalusia.

p. 61, stage direction, 'the Inquisition'. The Spanish Inquisition was founded in order to discover Jewish and Muslim converts to Christianity who secretly clung to their original beliefs.

Scene II

p. 62, stage direction, 'St James of Spain'. St James the Apostle, especially venerated in Spain, his remains are believed to be interred at Santiago de Compostela ('St James of Compostela') in Galicia, a major place of pilgrimage in the Middle Ages.

p. 63. Compare the story in 'Michael Clancy and the Great Dhoul and Death': W.B. Yeats, *Irish Folklore, Legend and Myth*, ed. Robert Welch (Harmondsworth: Penguin, 1993), pp. 100–7 (p. 106).

Scene III

p. 64, stage direction, '*auto-da-fé*'. In the Inquisition, the Church's ceremonial passing of sentence on those found guilty of heresy.

p. 69   'How Ferencz Renyi Kept Silent'

In 1848, one of a number of revolutions in Europe was that of the Hungarians, lasting until 1849, against the domination of Austria in the Austro-Hungarian Empire. Ferencz Renyi was a hero of this revolution. The imperial power exacted stern retribution.

'the Hungary of the West'. i.e., Ireland, under the domination of Britain, as Hungary was under that of Austria.

'Julius Jacob von Haynau' (1786–1853). A brilliant general in the Austrian army, notorious for his brutality.

p. 74   'Miserrimus'

Better known by its title in subsequent collections, 'The Sad Shepherd'.

p. 81   'On Mr Nettleship's Picture at the Royal Hibernian Academy'

The mission of the Royal Hibernian Academy, founded in 1823, is to promote and foster the arts, in a manner comparable to the Royal Academy in Britain. The painting is *Refuge*, by an English painter, J.T. Nettleship (1841–1902). He was a member of a group of artists called 'The Brotherhood', which included Yeats's father and Edwin Ellis, co-editor with Yeats of the great three-volume edition of Blake (1893). The picture shows a lion, and a lioness with her cub. They have fled to a rocky peak in order to seek refuge from a fire, which is visible in the background. Despite their situation, the lioness licks her cub.

p. 82   'A Legend'
Refers to a legend about Lough Gill, most of which is in Co. Sligo, though parts are in Co. Leitrim.

p. 83   'An Old Song Re-sung'
Best known as 'Down by the Salley Gardens'. The song to which Yeats refers in the title and note is in fact 'Ye Rambling Boys of Pleasure' (or some version of it), a well known song from the north of Ireland.

p. 86   'Quatrains and Aphorisms'
p. 87, 'Brahma'. See note to p. 45, 'Jealousy' (above).
'Sophocles'. The ancient Athenian playwright, who lived c.496–406 BCE.
'Attic'. Of or pertaining to Attica, the part of Greece of which Athens was chief city.

p. 91   'Island of Statues'
p. 100, 'the Wanderer'. Aeneas, who fled Troy after its fall, according to Virgil's Roman epic, *The Aeneid*. We can deduce his identity from the reference to Dido in the following line.
'I saw him from sad Dido's shore's depart'. Dido, Queen of Carthage according to Virgil, became the lover of Aeneas when his wanderings around the Mediterranean took him there. But he, charged with the destiny of founding a new city for his people, deserted her, and she was stricken by grief.
p. 101, 'Arthur – rule from Uther's chair'. King Arthur succeeded to the throne of his father, Uther Pendragon.
'Troia'. Troy.
'Achaians'. The Greeks are so termed in Homer's *Iliad,* which describes their long siege of Troy, which eventually fell.

Legends and Lyrics (1892)

Epigraph: 'The souls are threshed ...'. This is misquoted from Blake's *Vala* (or *The Four Zoas*), c.1796–1807, which was indeed, as far as we know, unpublished. In volume 3 of *The Works of William Blake*, edited by Yeats and Edwin Ellis (London, 1893), the line is given as 'And all the Nations were threshed out, and the stars threshed from their husks' (*Four Zoas*, IX, l. 648).

p. 105   'To the Rose upon the Rood of Time'
The rose is an important symbol in Yeats's work, especially his early work.

It is a compound of various associations. That the rose should be on a cross (or 'rood') reminds one of the occult Rosicrucian doctrines and rituals in which Yeats was an initiate in the Hermetic Order of the Golden Dawn, a magical order with masonic connections which he joined in 1890. The word 'Rosicrucian' was interpreted as referring to the rose and the cross. The symbolism of this conjunction, as Yeats understood it, is elaborated in this poem: the cross, which has connotations of the cross of Christ, symbolises the world of time, with all its struggle and suffering, but also the fact that out of suffering may come beauty – 'Eternal Beauty' (l. 12). This fact is further symbolised by the rose. It makes sense, then, that the reference to 'boughs of love and hate', in line 10, should equate the cross with a tree. The 'love and hate' remind us that life is made up of contrariety. But in the light of the references to ancient Irish tradition, it seems that the rose must also have national, or even nationalist, connotations. This would be borne out by the fact that the ancient dynasty of Ulster was known as 'the Red Branch'. In more modern times, there is an anonymous visionary nationalist poem, dating from the penal period, called 'Mo Róisín Dubh' ('My Little Dark Rose'), which personifies Ireland as a girl compared to or named after the rose. The best-known translation of this was 'My Dark Rosaleen', by the Irish poet James Clarence Mangan (1803–49). See also Yeats's own note at the end of *Legends and Lyrics*.

'Cuchullin'. See note to p. 109, 'The Death of Cuchullin' (below).

'Fergus'. See note to p. 29, 'Blanid', 'The Wanderings of Oisin' (above).

p. 106 · 'Fergus and the Druid'
For Fergus see note to p. 29, 'Blanid', 'The Wanderings of Oisin'(above). Druids were the priesthood of ancient Celtic peoples, and thus of Britain and Gaul as well as of Ireland. Yeats and his contemporaries were persuaded that ancient Celtic religion had pantheistic elements, and this was related to the capacity of Druids and other magically endowed beings to enter into different forms of life. These ideas are particularly relevant to the opening and closing lines of the poem.

'Red Branch'. Emblem of the kings of Ulster and their knights.

'Concobar'. Elsewhere 'Conor' or 'Conchubar', king of Ulster.

p. 108 'The Rose of the World'
'Usna', or more properly 'Usnach'. He had three sons, one of whom, Naoise, or Naisi, fell in love with Deirdre, and she with him. But King Conchubar coveted Deirdre for himself. The brothers fled with Deirdre to Scotland, but were tricked into returning. Conchubar arranged their deaths, including that of Naoise, and Deirdre committed suicide. This story is the basis for Yeats's play, *Deirdre* (1907).

p. 109 'The Death of Cuchullin'

Cuchullin (or Cuchulain, or more properly Cú Chulainn) is the champion warrior of Ulster in the cycle of sagas and tales revolving around the court of Ulster at Emain Macha, of which the most ambitious and best-known is *Táin Bó Cuailgne*, 'The Cattle-Raid of Cooley'. The present poem does not agree with the main lines of the tradition about Cuchulain, as his death is normally held to have occurred in a battle with Lugaid mac con Roí, who acts on the instigation of Queen Maeve of Connacht, and who has the assistance of trickery. In his note, given in the text, Yeats says, 'My poem is founded on a West of Ireland legend given by Curtin in "Myths and Folk lore of Ireland." The bardic tale of the death of Cuchullin is very different.' (Jeremiah Curtin [1838–1906] published that book in 1890.) In his later play, *The Death of Cuchulain* (1939), Yeats draws on the better-established tradition. However, at the heart of the current poem is an event, namely Cuchulain's mistakenly killing his only son, which is described in ancient sources as causing him to suffer such wild grief as to make him fight the waves of the sea, and this Yeats does represent. But in the ancient sources, this is followed by his suffering from a 'wasting sickness', and does not cause his death.

'Emer of Borda'. Cuchulain's wife.

'dun'. A fort, or fortified homestead.

p. 110, 'her son, Finmole'. At this stage in his reading of Irish tradition, Yeats seems not to have realised that it identifies Aoife as the mother, and not his wife Emer. Aoife was a warrior woman of Skye, from whom Cuchulain learnt the art of battle. See also Yeats's play, *On Baile's Strand* (1904).

'bitter'. Emer is bitter because of Cuchulain's infatuation with his young mistress (see l. 48).

'Red Branch kings'. See note to p. 105, 'To the Rose Upon the Rood of Time' (above).

'his young dear one'. Cuchulain's mistress, Eithne Inguba (as in Yeats's play, *The Only Jealousy of Emer* [1919]).

p. 111, 'Concobar'. See note to p. 106, 'Fergus and the Druid' (above).

p. 112 'The White Birds'

'Danaan'. Pertaining to the Tuatha Dé Danann: the Sidhe, the fairies.

p. 113 'Father Gilligan'

'Mavrone'. A cry of grief: Irish *mo bhrón*.

p. 115 'Father O'Hart'

'penal days'. The Penal Laws were punitive and oppressive laws imposed upon Irish Catholics from the 1690s, in contravention of the terms of the Treaty of Limerick (1691), which had terminated the struggle in which the forces of the Catholic monarch, James II, were defeated in Ireland. They were gradually repealed between the late eighteenth and the early nineteenth century.

'shoneen'. A transliteration of Irish Seoinín, from Irish Seon, which is the convention for English 'John'. The ending -ín ('een') is a diminutive, so a 'shoneen' is 'a little English John', used contemptuously of a man who affects English ways. (The normal Irish for John is Seán, pronounced 'Shawn'.)

'Sleiveens'. Sly people.

'Keeners', 'keening'. 'Keening' was ritual lamentation at a funeral. It consisted of wailing, crying and the recitation of verses of grief and commemoration.

'Coloony'. Collooney, a village in Co. Sligo.

p. 116, 'Knocknarea'. A mountain near Sligo.

'Knocknashee'. A hill in Co. Sligo.

'Tiraragh'. A barony in Co. Sligo.

'Ballinafad'. A village in Co. Sligo.

'Innismurry'. An island off the coast of Co. Sligo.

p. 116 'When You Are Old'

A free version, by no means a faithful translation, of 'Quand vous serez bien vieille', one of the *Sonnets pour Hélène* by the French poet Pierre de Ronsard (1524–85).

p. 119 'A Fairy Song'

Subtitle: 'the Good People'. The Sidhe, the fairies: a cautious euphemism for these dangerous beings. Michael Dwyer, of Co. Wicklow, was a leader in the 1798 rebellion. He was supposed to have escaped into the mountains with his bride.

p. 120 'The Lake Isle of Innisfree'

Innishfree (Inis Fraoigh, 'Island of Heather'), an island near the southern shore of Lough Gill, Co. Sligo.

p. 121 'A Cradle Song'

Epigraph: 'Coth yanni me von gilli beg, / 'N heur ve thu more a creena'. From a Gaelic lullaby sung by an old nurse in Gerald Griffin's novel *The Collegians* (1829). This is not, however, orthodox Gaelic spelling: the lines have been transcribed according to English phonetic conventions. Griffin gives the translation 'What will I do without my little darling / When you're grown up and old'.

'old planets seven'. i.e., the planets as understood in ancient times: Mercury, Venus, the Sun, the Moon, Mars, Jupiter and Saturn.

p. 121   'The Man who Dreamed of Fairyland'

'Drumahair'. Dromahair, a village in Co. Leitrim, not that far from Sligo.
p. 122, 'Lisadill'. Lissadell, an area near the sea north of Sligo. Lissadell House was the home of the Gore Booth family. Yeats was friendly with Constance (1868–1927) and Eva (1870–1926).
'Danaan'. See note to p. 112, 'The White Birds' (above).
'Scanavin'. In Co. Sligo.
'Lugnagall'. Townland at the mouth of the valley of Glencar, Co. Sligo.

p. 123   'Dedication of "Irish Tales"'

Yeats's *Representative Irish Tales* came out in 1891, an edited volume of tales by various Irish authors.
'green branch ... bell'. See note to p. 28, 'The Wanderings of Oisin' (above).
'Eri'. See note to p. 19, 'The Wanderings of Oisin' (above).

p. 124   'The Lamentation of the Old Pensioner'

'fret'. Agitation of mind; constant distress.

p. 127   'They Went Forth to the Battle, But They Always fell'

Better known by its title in subsequent collections, 'The Rose of Battle'. A misquotation of a phrase from *The Poems of Ossian* (1773), 'Cath-Loda', Duan ii, by James Macpherson (1736–96): 'they came forth to war, but they always fell'. Matthew Arnold (1822–88) quoted the phrase, in the form given by Yeats, in his lectures *On Celtic Literature*, a work well known to Yeats, to illustrate a truth about the Celtic temperament.

p. 128   'Apologia Addressed to Ireland in the Coming Days'

Better known by its title in subsequent collections, 'To Ireland in the Coming Times'.
'rann'. Irish: a stanza.
p. 129, 'Davis, Mangan, Ferguson'. Thomas Davis (1814–45), Irish political leader, writer and poet; James Clarence Mangan (1803–49), Irish poet; Sir Samuel Ferguson (1810–86), Irish poet.

p. 130   Yeats's Notes to *Legends and Lyrics*

'To the Rose upon the Rood of Time'
'De Vere'. Aubrey de Vere (1840–1902), poet and man of letters.
'Mangan'. James Clarence Mangan (1803–49), Irish poet.

'Father O'Hart'
'Coloony'. Collooney, a village in Co. Sligo.

'The Ballad of the Old Fox Hunter'
'Kickham's "Knocknagow"'. Charles J. Kickham (1828–82) was the author of the nationalist novel *Knocknagow* (1873).

The Wind Among the Reeds (1899)

p. 133 'The Hosting of the Sidhe'
For 'Sidhe', see note to p. 3, the subtitle of 'The Wanderings of Oisin' (above), and see Yeats's own note at the end of *The Wind Among the Reeds*.
'Knocknarea'. A mountain south of Sligo. Queen Maeve is reputed to be buried under a cairn at its summit. And see Yeats's own note.
'Clooth-na-bare'. See Yeats's own lengthy note, in which he explains that this name is a corruption of 'Cailleac Bare', the 'old woman of Bare', and that, being also one of the Sidhe, she had grown weary of her life, probably because the Sidhe can never die.
'Caolte'. Often spelt 'Caoilte'. One of the companions of Finn mac Cumhaill.
'Niamh'. The same as the fairy enchantress 'Niam' in the 1889 version of 'The Wanderings of Oisin'.

p. 134 'Aedh Tells of the Rose in his Heart'
Aedh is one of several personae adopted by Yeats in this volume, and subsequently erased, being replaced with the mere pronoun 'he'. Yeats explains, in the note on 'Aedh', 'Hanrahan' and 'Michael Robartes', that Aedh is both the Irish equivalent of Hugh, and 'the Irish for fire'. In *The Wind Among the Reeds* it is said to represent 'fire burning by itself', which is further explained as 'the myrrh and frankincense that the imagination offers continually before all that it loves'. Certainly, 'Aodh' (*sic*) is the Irish for 'Hugh' and is understood to mean 'fire', though the normal modern Irish word for fire is *tine*.

p. 135 'The Host of the Air'
Another way of referring to the Sidhe, or fairies. See also Yeats's notes following the poems.

p. 136 'Breasal the Fisherman'
Probably in part a reflection of Yeats's knowledge of the tale *Echtra Bhresail*, 'The Adventures of Bresal', recounted in the medieval *Book of Leinster*, and retold in *Silva Gadelica*, by Standish Hayes O'Grady (1832–1915), a work

with which Yeats was familiar. Bresal dives into Loch Laoigh, and remains under the waves for fifty years. The emphasis on fishing (albeit figuratively understood) in this poem was confirmed when Yeats changed the title to 'The Fisherman' from 1906 onwards, and then to 'The Fish' from 1933.

p. 137 'A Cradle Song'
'Danann children'. The children of the fairies.
'unappeasable host'. A reference to the fairies again.
'Maurya'. English phonetic rendition of Irish Máire ('Mary'): a reference to the Virgin Mary. This is just one of many indications of Yeats's uncertain grasp of Irish, since the Blessed Virgin is normally given a special version of this name, spelt Muire (pronounced 'Mweera').

p. 137 'Into the Twilight'
In its first printing, in *The National Observer* (1893), the title was 'The Celtic Twilight'.

p. 138 'The Song of Wandering Aengus'
Aengus, one of the Sidhe, was in 1895 described by Yeats as 'the god of youth, beauty and poetry'. See also Yeats's own note on this poem.
'hazel'. A magical wood in Irish tradition.

p. 139 'The Fiddler of Dooney'
Dooney Rock on the shores of Lough Gill.
'Kilvarnet', 'Moharabuiee'. Kilvarnet and Maugheraboy are places in Co. Sligo.

p. 140 'Aedh Laments the Loss of Love'
For 'Aedh' see note to p. 134, 'Aedh Tells of the Rose in his Heart' (above).

p. 141 'Mongan Laments the Change that has Come upon him and his Beloved'
Mongan, as Yeats pointed out in a note to 'Mongan Thinks of his Past Greatness', was 'a famous wizard and king who remembers his past lives'. This is another version of 'Celtic' transmigration of souls, and probably of Druidism as well. The most illustrious of Mongan's past lives, however, was as none other than Finn mac Cumhaill, as we discover in Kuno Meyer and Alfred Nutt's translation of the romance *The Voyage of Bran Son of Febal to the Land of the Living*, 2 vols. (1895, 1897), vol. I (1895), p. 52.
'hound with one red ear'. See Yeats's entry on this poem in his notes.
'hazel wand'. Hazel is a magical wood in Irish tradition.
'boar without bristles'. See Yeats's entry in his notes for 'The Valley of the

Black Pig', where he identifies the boar that killed Diarmuid, the lover of Gráinne in a well-known medieval romance, as having no bristles. The boar appears to be an emblem of death and chaos.

p. 141   'Michael Robartes Bids his Beloved Be at Peace'
In his note on the personae of *The Wind Among the Reeds*, Yeats states that Robartes is 'fire reflected in water', or 'the pride of the imagination brooding upon the greatness of its possessions'.
'Shadowy Horses'. The Fomorians, or spirits of darkness, arrive on ghostly horses. See Yeats's note.

p. 142   'Hanrahan Reproves the Curlew'
First published in *The Savoy* (November, 1896), with the title 'Windle-straws / I. O'Sullivan Rua to the Curlew'. A windle-straw is a dry, thin, withered stalk of grass. The term might be applied figuratively to a weak or feeble person or thing: this fact may indicate a link with the title of the eventual collection, *The Wind Among the Reeds*. 'O'Sullivan Rua' is Owen Roe (or Rua) O'Sullivan (Eoghan Ruadh Ó Súilleabháin, 1748–84), an Irish-language poet from Co. Kerry, who wrote, among other things, *aisling* (vision) poems: that is, poems in which the speaker experiences a vision of a fair woman who personifies Ireland. *Ruadh* (reformed spelling [1948], *rua*) is the Irish for red, and it should be noted that Hanrahan, who replaces O'Sullivan in the title, is elsewhere called 'Red Hanrahan' by Yeats. ('Windle-straws II', subtitled 'Out of the Old Days', is the poem that became 'To my Heart, Bidding it Have No Fear' in 1899, and subsequently 'To his Heart […]'.)

p. 142   'Michael Robartes Remembers Forgotten Beauty'
For Michael Robartes, see note to p. 141, 'Michael Robartes Bids his Beloved be at Peace' (above).

p. 143   'Aedh Gives his Beloved Certain Rhymes'
For 'Aedh' see note to p. 134, 'Aedh Tells of the Rose in his Heart' (above).

p. 145   'The Valley of the Black Pig'
Yeats's entry for this poem in his notes is very informative.
'cromlec'. Usually spelt 'cromlech': a prehistoric stone edifice, consisting of a horizontal stone slab held aloft by vertical stone slabs creating what looks like a kind of doorway, though it will probably have been the covering for the inner chamber of a burial mound.

p. 146 'Michael Robartes Asks Forgiveness Because of his Many Moods'
For Michael Robartes, see note to p. 141, 'Michael Robartes bids his Beloved be at Peace' (above).

p. 147 'Aedh Tells of a Valley Full of Lovers'
For 'Aedh' see note to p. 134, 'Aedh Tells of the Rose in his Heart' (above).

p. 147 'Aedh Tells of the Perfect Beauty'
For 'Aedh' see note to p. 134, 'Aedh Tells of the Rose in his Heart' (above).

p. 148 'Aedh Hears the Cry of the Sedge'
For 'Aedh' see note to p. 134, 'Aedh Tells of the Rose in his Heart' (above).

p. 148 'Aedh Thinks of Those who have Spoken Evil of his Beloved'
For 'Aedh' see note to p. 134, 'Aedh Tells of the Rose in his Heart' (above).

p. 149 'The Blessed'
'Cumhal'. In Yeats's short story, 'The Crucifixion of the Outcast', collected in *The Secret Rose* (1897), Cumhal is a wandering bard.
'Dathi'. In Yeats's short story 'The Crucifixion of the Outcast', collected in *The Secret Rose* (1897), Dathi is a remnant of the pagan Celtic order.

p. 150 'The Secret Rose'
'Holy Sepulchre'. The tomb of Christ.
'Magi'. Persian wise men and magicians, three of whom were supposed to have visited the infant Jesus.
'the king'. According to Yeats's note, Conchubar, who converted to Christianity.
'Pierced Hands and Rood'. The hands of Christ, pierced by the nails which fixed him to the cross, or rood.
'and him / Who met Fand'. Cuchulain, who fell in love with Fand, a woman of the Sidhe, forgetting his love for his wife, Emer.
'Emer', wife of Cuchulain.
'him who drove the gods out of their liss'. Caoilte, a companion of Finn mac Cumhail; a 'liss' (Irish *lios*) is a small mound or barrow, popularly believed to be inhabited by the Sidhe (the Tuatha Dé Danann, the fairies).
p. 151, 'proud dreaming king'. Fergus. See note to p. 29, 'Blanid', 'The Wanderings of Oisin' (above).
'him who sold tillage'. Refers to a character in 'The Red Pony', a story by William Larminie (1849–1900).

p. 151   'Hanrahan Laments because of his Wanderings'
For 'Hanrahan', see note to p. 142, 'Hanrahan Reproves the Curlew' (above).

p. 152   'The Travail of Passion'
'scourge [...], 'plaited thorns' [...], 'wounds in palm and side' [...], 'hyssop-heavy sponge': all references to the crucifixion of Christ, including the sponge, which is used to moisten his lips on the cross: 'Now there was set a vessel full of vinegar: and they filled a spunge with vinegar, and put it upon hyssop, and put it to his mouth' (King James Bible, John 19:29).
'Kidron'. The brook that flows between Jerusalem and the Mount of Olives: another reference to the crucifixion.

p. 153   'Hanrahan Speaks to the Lovers of his Songs in Coming Days'
For 'Hanrahan', see note to p. 142, 'Hanrahan Reproves the Curlew' (above).
'O, colleens'. *Cailín* ('colleen') is the Irish (and Scottish) Gaelic for a girl.
'Maurya'. See note to p. 137, 'A Cradle Song' (above).

p. 153   'Aedh Pleads with the Elemental Powers'
For 'Aedh' see note to p. 134, 'Aedh Tells of the Rose in his Heart' (above).
'Seven Lights'. The seven stars of the Great Bear or Plough.
'The Polar Dragon'. The constellation of Draco, the Dragon, close to the
    Pole Star.

p. 154   'Aedh Wishes his Beloved were Dead'
For 'Aedh' see note to p. 134, 'Aedh Tells of the Rose in his Heart' (above).

p. 154   'Aedh Wishes for the Cloths of Heaven'
For 'Aedh' see note to p. 134, 'Aedh Tells of the Rose in his Heart' (above).

p. 155   'Mongan Thinks of his Past Greatness'
For Mongan, see note to p. 141, 'Mongan Laments the Change that has Come upon him and his Beloved' (above).
'the Country of the Young'. Tír na nÓg, home of the immortal Sidhe or
    fairies.
'hazel tree'. A magical tree in Irish tradition.
'The Pilot Star and the Crooked Plough'. The Pole Star and the Plough (or
    Great Bear), the one at the height of the heavens, the other near it. Thus,
    the Tree of Life reaches to heaven.

p. 156   Yeats's Notes to *The Wind Among the Reeds*

'The Hosting of the Sidhe'

'Herodias'. A Jewish princess (*c*.15 BCE–*c*.39 CE), supposed in the Middle Ages to be the leader of a witchcraft cult.

'Kiltartan'. In Co. Galway.

'Lomna, the fool of Fiann'. A foolish associate of the Fianna, or the warriors who followed Finn mac Cumhail.

'Tristram […] Tristram and Iseult'. Refers to the Arthurian tale of the ill-fated love of the Cornish knight Tristram (or Tristan) and the Irish princess Iseult (or Isolde).

'The Celtic Twilight'. Yeats's *The Celtic Twilight* (first edition, 1893), a collection of Irish folk tales and traditions.

'Usheen'. Yeats sometimes used this phonetic spelling of Oisin.

'Mr O'Grady'. Standish James O'Grady (1846–1928).

'"Flight of the Eagle"'. Standish James O'Grady's *The Flight of the Eagle* (1897).

'Fionn'. The modern Irish form of Finn's name.

'Dr Joyce'. P.W. Joyce (1827–1914), author of *Old Celtic Romances* (1879).

'Aebhen'. More correctly, Aoibheall: a goddess of north Munster.

'Clontarf'. On the coast north of Dublin, the site of a major battle of 1014 in which the armies of the High King Brian Boru decisively defeated the Vikings of Dublin.

'Aedh Pleads with the Elemental Powers', 'Mongan Thinks of his Past Greatness', 'Aedh Hears the Cry of the Sedge'

'Count Goblet D'Alviella'. Eugène Félicien Albert, Count Goblet d'Alviella (1846–1925). Belgian lawyer, freemason, student of religions and religious symbolism.

'Apuleius' (*c*.123/125–*c*.180 CE). Author of a fabulous tale *The Golden Ass*, to which Yeats refers.

'Dr Hyde'. Douglas Hyde (1860–1949), scholar, translator of Irish poetry, first President of Ireland (1938–45).

'Mangan'. See note to 'Apologia addressed to Ireland in the Coming Days' (above).

'Aubrey de Vere'. (1840–1902), poet and man of letters.

'Dr Joyce'. See notes on Yeats's note to 'The Hosting of the Sidhe' (above).

'Arann'. i.e., the Isles of Aran, off the Galway coast.

'Burren hills'. Or 'the Burren', in Co. Clare. An area of limestone hills.

'The Song of Wandering Aengus'

'Burren'. See previous note.

'*Michael Robartes Bids his Beloved Be at Peace*'
'Fomor'. Or 'Fomorians' (Irish, Fomoire). They are much as Yeats describes
  them.
'Mannannan'. Manannán mac Lir, presumed to have been the pre-Christian
  Irish god of the sea.
'Tethra'. A king of the Fomorians who dwelt underground.

'*Mongan Laments the Change that has Come upon him and his Beloved*',
'*Hanrahan Laments because of his Wanderings*'
'Annwvyn'. Annwfn, the Welsh underworld.
'Setanta' was Cuchulain's original name. He received the name Cú Chulainn
  after he himself (not his son) killed the hound of the guard Culann, after
  it attacked him. The confusion may arise because Yeats may regard
  'Setanta' as a kind of patronymic.
'Professor Rhys'. John Rhys, in *Lectures on the Origin and Growth of Religion
  as Illustrated by Celtic Heathendom* (1888).
'Salome'. Daughter of King Herod Antipas, who danced before him, prior
  to demanding, at her mother's behest, the head of John the Baptist.
'Land League'. An Irish political organisation of the later nineteenth century
  which agitated for the right of tenant farmers to own the land on which
  they worked.
'Lisadell'. See note to p. 122, 'The Man who Dreamed of Fairyland' (above).
'Dearmod'. i.e., Diarmuid, in the romance of Diarmuid and Gráinne, who
  was killed by a boar.
'Ben Bulben'. Mountain to the north of Sligo.
'Misroide MacDatha's sow'. Yeats is referring to the Old Irish tale of
  MacDathó's pig. When it was killed and roasted for a feast, there were
  great quarrels over who should carve it first, followed by a battle.
'Celtic Heathendom'. *Lectures on the Origin and Growth of Religion as Illustrated
  by Celtic Heathendom* by John Rhys (1888).
'Adonis'. Ancient god of near-eastern origins, whose cult was popular in
  classical times. He was gored to death by a boar.
'Attis'. Ancient god from Phrygia in Asia Minor (modern Turkey). He was
  the lover of Cybele, but was unfaithful to her. She drove him mad, and
  he castrated himself.
'Golden Bough'. *The Golden Bough: A Study in Magic and Religion*, a work
  of comparative mythology and anthropology by Sir James George Frazer
  (1854–1941). First published in two volumes in 1890, it had expanded
  to twelve by the time of the third edition, published 1906–15.
'Courland'. An ancient province of Latvia.
'Professor Rhys'. Author of *Lectures on the Origin and Growth of Religion as
  Illustrated by Celtic Heathendom*. See 'Celtic Heathendom', above.

'Moy Tura'. Moytura in Co. Sligo.

'The Secret Rose'
'Conchobar'. Or Conchubar, or Conor, King of Ulster in the heroic age.
'Keating'. Geoffrey Keating (or Seathrún Céitinn), DD (*c.*1569–*c.*1644), author of *Foras Feasa ar Éirinn* ('A History of Ireland', *c.*1634).
'Fand'. See note to p. 150, 'The Secret Rose': 'and him / Who met Fand' (above).
'Uladh'. Ulster.
'Mannannan'. See note to Yeats's note on 'Michael Roberts Bids his Beloved Be at Peace', above.
'Caolte'. Or 'Caoilte', one of the companions of Finn.
'battle of Gabra'. The Battle of Gabhra brought to an end the glory of Finn and his warrior companions (or Fianna).
'Ossory'. Ancient Irish kingdom centred on what is now Co. Kilkenny.
'Ballyshannon'. Town in Co. Donegal.
'Fergus'. See note to p. 29, 'Blanid', 'The Wanderings of Oisin' (above).
'the quest of the bull of Cualge'. Yeats means the Old Irish epic saga *Táin Bó Cuailgne*, 'The Cattle Raid of Cooley'.
'Ferguson'. Sir Samuel Ferguson (1810–86), Irish poet.
'Fergus and the Druid'. From *Legends and Lyrics*, included above in this collection.
'The Countess Kathleen'. Yeats's play, first published in *The Countess Kathleen and Various Legends and Lyrics* in 1892. Subsequently revised and spelt *The Countess Cathleen*. The Countess sells her soul to the demons in return for gold with which she intends to save the people from starvation in the Famine. Nevertheless, her soul is saved, because God considers the intention behind our actions.
'Mr Larminie's "West Irish Folk Tales"'. William Larminie (1849–1900), *West Irish Folk Tales* (1893).

Index of Titles

Index of First Lines